The Wonder of the Tao

The Wonder of the Tao

of the Tao

A Meditation on Spirituality & Ecological Balance

James Eggert
Foreword by Thich Nhat Hanh

Humanics Trade Group
Atlanta -- Lake Worth

HUMANICS

The Wonder of the Tao
A Humanics Trade Group Publication
© 2004 by Brumby Holdings, Inc.
First Edition

Humanics Trade Group Publications is an imprint of and published by Humanics Publishing Group, a division of Brumby Holdings, Inc. Its trademark, consisting of the words "Humanics Trade Group" and the portrayal of a pegasus, is registered in the U.S. Patent and Trademark Office and in other countries.

Illustrations & Calligraphy by Li-chin (Crystal) Huang

Brumby Holdings, Inc.
12 S. Dixie Hwy, Ste. 200
Lake Worth, FL 33460
USA

Printed in the United States of America and the United Kingdom

ISBN (Paperback) 0-89334-397-8
ISBN (Hardcover) 0-89334-398-6

Library of Congress Control Number: 2003115282

for Patricia

Table of Contents

Foreword

James Eggert offers us an engaging and poetic meditation on responsibility and interbeing. On the east coast of the USA we have the Statue of Liberty. Perhaps we should consider erecting a statue of responsibility on the west coast to remind us of our responsibility to each other and to our precious earth. Compassionate living is cultivated on the ground of understanding. It is possible to contribute to reducing the violence and destruction in our world with our everyday actions. A step taken in mindfulness, a gentle smile is already an act of peace, an act of compassion. Understanding deeply our inseparable connectedness with the natural world, with the trees, the sunshine and the fresh air, we will know how to protect and how to take care of our precious planet, our home.

Please enjoy this offering of our friend, James Eggert, as an invitation to enter into a deep relationship with our home the earth and all her creatures, to cultivate our awakened wisdom to find harmony and balance.

Thich Nhat Hanh
Green Lake Wisconsin
August, 28th, 2003

Preface

I'm wondering: have you ever — perhaps for a brief moment — felt an unmistakable joy in the midst of nature?

Or awe? Or, as Einstein once wrote, a feeling of "rapturous" amazement with the Universe — its parts, its wholeness and its unfathomable mystery?

If so, you may have experienced the momentary rebirth of an ancient consciousness resonating with the same delight, the same natural pleasure of the God of *Genesis* who, (like a deep ecologist), proclaimed that His Creation was not only good, but "very good." Surely such moments are worth sharing and celebrating.

But have you also felt that sense of loss and depression (or anger) that so much of the natural world is literally disappearing before our eyes: landscapes disfigured, wildlife slaughtered, or once clear and clean waters polluted? Add in sprawl, smog, and commercial/electronic "noise," species extinctions, ozone depletions, tropical rainforest degradations, and the growing evidence of climatic alterations. "Celebration and Loss" are thus the major themes of Part I.

If there is ever to be a lasting rebirth of environmental consciousness, I believe it will come not with conflict, arguments, or even intellectual analysis, but more in the small rivulets and tributaries of our personal experiences, thoughts, and affections. These in turn flow into stories and conversations and then continue on into the broader flowage of principles, and values.

The one principle most in mind in Part II is the ancient Chinese ideal of balance. At the personal level, we will take a couple chapters (IV and V) to explore the quality of yin/yang energy balance as expressed in the practice of the Chinese martial art T'ai Chi.

Meanwhile, Chapter 6 ("The Wonder of the Tao") briefly explores "balance" within a broader framework of religion, culture, and economics. As an example, a Taiwanese economist recently asked me: "How can my country apply the principle of Taoist balance to Capitalism and economic growth?"

Granted, there's an uplift of living standards when market forces are unleashed. Indeed, few can deny the raw volcanic power of for-profit capitalism. Yet how often does its "volcano" spread it's lava over landscapes, habitats, values and indigenous cultures? Put at the simplest level, Taiwan's economy must find a balance — with policies, investments, and patterns of consumption — that guarantee the preservation of essential ecosystems, including fresh waters, soils, forests, fisheries, wildlife habitat, as well as the country's beautiful and sacred, story-filled landscapes.

It must also be balanced by a commitment to preserve indigenous cultures and encourage local sustainable practices. And finally, (again using Taiwan as an example), centralized political power must be balanced by individual and community self-determination, of empowering people with the conviction and fact of democracy. The principle of "balance" can, I believe, waft its healing aroma and corrective powers into many of our Twenty-First Century's most perplexing and dangerous dilemmas.

I will begin however, not by drawing up new theories or large-scale solutions — but with my own "rivulet" of experience and affection, of kneeling down one lovely fall morning to a miniature world of mushrooms and spider webs.

Acknowledgements

A warm "thank you" to those friends, relatives, and colleagues who offered me encouragement on this project and especially to those who generously provided ideas, additions, subtractions, or clarifying modifications to the book's early drafts.

More specifically I would like to thank Bea Bigony, John Williams, my wife Pat Eggert, Joe Johnson, Dave Bauer, Mari Rose, Larry Lynch, Nan Becker, Stan Smith, Bob Evans, Becky Simonson, Chuck Sorensen, Lee Smalley, artist and calligrapher Crystal Huang, Parker Huber, Peggy Brace, Ken Salway, Kenneth Cohen, Paul Wyss, son Anthony and daughter Leslie, Connie Baxter Marlow, Arnie Neptune, Joe Plouff, Ken Parejko, economists Bob Eggert Sr. and Professor Jason Shih, as well as my T'ai Chi mentors David Chang, Ming Hsien Huang, and Benjamin Pang Jeng Lo. Again, a heart-felt thanks to each and every one of you.

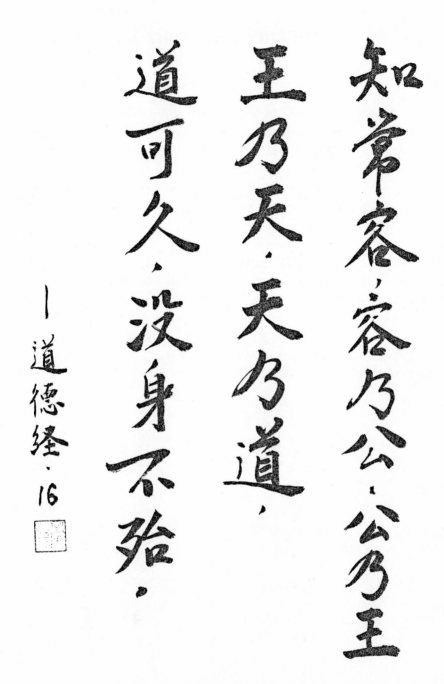

知常容，容乃公，公乃王

王乃天，天乃道，

道可久，没身不殆，

—道德经·16

"Immersed in the Wonder of the Tao..."

When you realize where you come from,
you naturally become tolerant,
disinterested, amused,
kindhearted as a grandmother,
dignified as a king.
Immersed in the wonder of the Tao,
you can deal with whatever life brings you,
and when death comes, you are ready.

Lao Tzu: *Tao Te Ching*[1]

Part 1
Celebration and Loss

"eleven mushrooms"

Chapter 1
Life!

Tao is in an ant, in a blade of grass, in a roof tile, in dung...
you'll not find it apart from the ten thousand things."[2]
Chung Tzu

A little "miracle" comes our way, ever so rarely, rising up out of a bed of pine needles, here on our pin-oak/jack-pine savanna soils of west-central Wisconsin. I drop to my knees.

The atmosphere is quiet. The pine-duff layer seems soft and moist to the palm of my hand. There, glossy in the low morning sun, is a fist-sized ring of tiny mushrooms — *Panaeolus foenesecii* — all eleven of them brightened by fresh sunlight beaming through the pine boughs. Each is vigorous, healthy — full of *mirth* it seems to me. Bending down, I touch one with my cheek: cool in temperature, rubbery to the skin, it's packed with a "new-born life-force" one might say. Closer to the ground now, I suddenly see small strands of spider webs rippling to my right, each fluttering in ruffled waves of rainbow color.

Consider for a moment the favorable confluence of historic and current conditions — biological, geological, atmospheric — first to *conceive* of this scene and then to make it into a solid *fact*: air temperature, night-time humidity, morning sun, perfect pine-duff moisture, plus all the necessary mushroom-producing nutrients. A delicate combination of chemistry and biology — of DNA imperatives hereby springing up *life!* and now spreading out before me in windpuffed riffles of color. Lost in wonder — as if submersed in a dilation of time — I sense old kinships in these familiar forms, an antique Creativity summoning up newfound energies. From primordial conditions to such beauty, "How" I wonder, "did the Universe do it?"

And *you* too (and myself yes), are we not equal partners of such processes, a "popping-up" out of rare circumstances, a genuine gift arising from equally improbable events? Are we not (like the mush-rooms) exquisite outcomes of evolutionary forces from a truly creative Universe cooking up new flavors of recombinant matter, of compounds heated and shaped by fields of cosmic energies — both weak and strong — over unimaginable quantities of time? And what about Earth itself?

Rare Earth

Peter Ward and Donald Brownless in their book *Rare Earth*[3] argue that our planet, and especially its complex life, is likewise an extremely improbable event. If true (and their argument seems per-suasive), our species and its cultural/technological status, may be the *only* example of "our kind" within galactic range. Like the mush-rooms, our planet appears to be a result of a unique confluence of favorable factors. What are they? Indeed, why are such complex "liv-ing-earths" so rare? Let's take a moment to examine some of the main points.

First, our species required a planet that was situated in the "right" galactic neighborhood, one safely distanced — in the "suburbs" so to speak — from the deadly radiation of the central core's densely-packed neutron stars, supernovas, and a massive black hole at or near the center of the Milky Way. We also had to "choose" a planet resid-ing in an older galaxy, one that had been around sufficient time to recy-cle materials *into* birthing stars and *out of* dying novas and supernovas — each titanic explosion a cosmic factory for fusing simpler, lighter atoms into heavier elements: hydrogen to helium, on to carbon, oxy-gen, silicon, and iron, each transformation creating critical ingredients for life as we know it.[4]

Next, we had to "select" a planet with sufficient quantities of water and, not unlike the mushroom pine-duff, a planetary mantle lib-erally sprinkled with such life-supporting compounds. We would also need a planet with some atmospheric oxygen plus a stratospheric ozone membrane. Like the gentle hands of a loving mother, Earth's precious ozone layer protects all her terrestrial "children" from the Sun's dead-ly ultraviolet radiation.

Equally important, we would require what astronomers have dubbed a "Goldilocks Planet" which, like the Little Bear's memorable porridge, was not "too hot" (like Venus), nor "too cold" (like Mars). Recall that wonderful moment — the one that always makes the children smile — in the *Three Bears* story:

> And then she [Goldilocks] went to the porridge of the Little Wee Bear, and tasted it, and that was neither too hot nor too cold, but just right, and she liked it so well, that she ate it all up, every bit![5]

Earth is, in fact, the *only* planet we know that enjoys an average global temperature within a comfortable, life-supporting range between the freezing and boiling point of water. The authors of *Rare Earth* also remind us of the importance of Earth's relatively large moon which helped stabilize our planet's tilt and life-supporting atmosphere. In addition, Earth would require a sizable "sibling," a planetary Big-Brother with a Jupiter-strength gravity sufficient to absorb dangerous interplanetary projectiles. Without Jupiter, we would have been pummeled much too often and thereby suffered too many mass extinctions over the past half-billion years.

Yet, ironically, *some* jolts and planet-wide buffetings would be necessary. According to the rare-earth hypothesis, the evolution of humans required episodes of ice-ages and also *some* (not too many) earth-shattering impacts from above. Consider the great dinosaur extinction of sixty-five million years ago which allowed furry, shrew-like mammals of the night (our ancestors) to get a foothold and then, over millions of years, to occupy new and safe daytime niches around the globe.

We would also require a planet that had the capacity to stir things up from below through plate-tectonics. Moving plates not only recycle essential chemicals, but continuously create novel habitats and new niche opportunities which, over relatively long periods of time, reshape bodies and behaviors into new species through the process of natural selection.

How lucky we are! Lucky to reside on a planet with tortoise-paced moving continents. Indeed, lucky to inhabit a possible one-in-a-billion "rare Earth" finely tuned for birthing such a wide range of bio-diversity.

獨愴然而淚下　念天地之悠悠　後不見來者　前不見古人

"Where are all the ancestors who I never met..."(See Appendix I)

That special morning was graced by mushrooms and resplendent spider-webs fluttering in the wind, and also by a unique rare earth species-consciousness invoking feelings of wonder and a renewed sense of *planetary preciousness*. But I also had a feeling of emptiness, or more accurately, of *cosmic loneliness*, of meandering about in a minor key. And who could not also feel a deepening fear, or a sense of *dread*, that our requisite care and tenderness toward our unique planet has not always been what it should, that the Earth has been so tampered with by human violence and ecosystem disfigurement? That our technologies and earth-consuming appetites have so altered the biosphere that many of those things we hold onto with such affection are now beginning to fade, seep away, indeed slip forever from our fingers?

Consider the "dying of the trees"[6] and forests, and the growing number of bleached-out coral reefs. Consider global warming, ozone thinning, or the world-wide shortages of fresh water.[7] Or the well-documented amphibian declines and deformities[8] (and the extinction of that beautiful, shimmering Golden Toad of the rain-forests of Costa Rica). With any species extinction — such as the passenger pigeon, dodo, great auk, heath hen, or dusky seaside sparrow, to name a few — one might pause and consider writer Mark Walter's observation that though death is the end of life, "extinction is the end of birth."[9] Another writer argues that "extinction kills...the soul as well as the body" and that "to superkill a species is to shut down a story of millennia and leave no future possibilities.[10]

We must also consider the world's bourgeoning human population — some six billion souls with all their material needs plus their pent-up desires — a population which, if current trends continue, will become half again as large within a generation. Consider too, the clear cutting of U.S. National Forests and Asian mountainsides, or the growing severity of worldwide droughts, and elsewhere, torrential rains and tragic mudslides cascading down and through cities,[11] villages, farms and fields.

Where, one might ask, are our "Rare-Earth" religions or "Rare-Earth" economics, or evidence of "Rare-Earth" political sensibilities encircling the globe?   Where's our commitment to a *Rare Earth Covenant* flowing from influential representatives of our society: science and religion, economics and business, dedicated to protecting Creation from plunder and defilement?

Surely many of the early spiritual traditions were both informed and enriched by environmental insights, while demonstrating a degree of ecological consciousness.   They transmitted to their followers a heightened appreciation of the Earth and an awareness of some deep, interconnected, harmonic chord of *all* life.   I think, for example, of that great prophetic verse from the Taoist spiritual classic, the *Tao Te Ching*, a verse that beautifully captures all the delicacy, fragility, indeed the vulnerability of the natural world, the wonder of Tao's "ten-thousand things"

> *Those who would take over the earth*
> *and shape it to their will,*
> *never, I notice, succeed.*
> *The earth is like a vessel so sacred*
> *that at the mere approach of the profane*
> *it is marred*
> *and when they reach out their fingers it is gone.*[12]

Or a passage in the final book of the *Bible*, a revelation startling perhaps to those who may have never considered this book a powerful environmental document:

> *...that thou should give reward unto thy servants*
> *the prophets...and should destroy*
> *them which destroy the earth.*[13]

Or listen to what may be the greatest deep ecology values-statement of all time — when the God of *Genesis* takes a moment to contemplate *everything* He has made and proclaims:

> *"...it was very good."*[14]

將欲取天下而為之，

吾見其不得已，

天下神器，不可為也，

為者敗之，執者失之

——道德経·29

"Those who would take over the earth..."

Consider too the story of Noah, especially its great moral teaching, which according to biologist Calvin DeWitt, is nothing more or less than the "world's first Endangered Species Act."[15] DeWitt reminds us that *Genesis* 6:9 highlights God's command that "Noah prevent the extinction of all creatures, *both economic and uneconomic*, no matter what the cost."[16]

Buddhists add an additional element of environmental awareness in the view that humans are not separate from the creation, but intimately part of it and *interdependent with it*. In his book, *The Sun My Heart*, Zen Buddhist monk Thich Nhat Hanh illustrates this relationship when he asks his readers to consider "the immense light we call the sun":

> If it stops shining, the flow of our life will also stop, and so the sun is our second heart, our heart outside of our body. This immense "heart" gives all life on earth the warmth necessary for existence, along with carbon dioxide from the air, to produce food for the tree, the flower, the plankton. And thanks to plants, we and other animals can live...We cannot begin to describe all the effects of the sun, that great heart out-side our body.[17]

Elsewhere he (Nhat Hanh) comments:

> Look into the self and discover that it is made only of non-self elements. A human being is made up of only non-human elements. To protect humans, we have to protect the non-human elements — the air, the water the forest, the river, the mountains, and the animals...Human can survive only with the survival of other species. This is exactly the teaching of the Buddha, and also the teaching of deep ecology.[18]

One's growing awareness of this Earth/human interdependence may therefore become a touchstone for one's behavior, life-style, and day-to-day choices.

Yet, for some reason, traditional environmental consciousness — both in the East and West — has become enfeebled, like a far-off candle light obscured by great and growing distances — as we race "forward" embracing the novelty of technology, "bottom-line" obsessions, and a far-ranging infectious consumerism — making all too many of us unwitting contributors to the slow but steady degradation of this beautiful planet and its countless wonders.

So *who* is responsible and why? I would, of course, like to point my finger outward — toward the obvious: corrupt governments, greedy transnationals, or perhaps to advertisers and media moguls whose vision of "paradise" is unalloyed materialism fueled by profits and exponential growth. But try as I might, all too often, my finger — if I am honest — points right back toward me.

天網恢恢
疏而不失

一道德経·74

"The Tao is like a vast net..."

Plum Blossoms

Chapter II
Co-Responsibility

The Tao is like a vast net.
Although its mesh is too large to be found,
Nothing can escape it.[19]

Jewels on Indra's net
Reflect each other endlessly.[20]

I recall so well that evening when — in the bloom of spring — my wife and I took a leisurely walk down a nearby nature trail. It was all ours for the seeing, the listening, and here and there, for the sweet smelling of the plum blossoms hanging over the path. On the edge of the trail, we found fresh floral offspring of botanical natives — of those ancestors who settled here before our time, their "great-grandchildren" now deeply rooted, as if with a sense of peace and belonging: juneberry, troutlily, and growing out of a wet bank, fronds of fern unfurling.

Soon we passed a prairie remnant and further on, we discovered marsh marigolds blooming in a sparkling bog. (Like the sacred Lotus of India, we have our own "marsh-golds" flaring their colors up out of the mud and into our hearts.) Nearby, skunk-cabbages sprouted little "elephant ears" for leaves, a Yellowthroat Warbler scolded "Whichity...Whichity," a Catbird "Meaaowed" from behind a bush. We paused. "What's that faint trill?"

What's that high-pitched, haunting trill — as if a thin string of beads had been lofted out of a wet meadow then transmuted, magically, into sound? Ah, it was the music of little toads, who like other lovers on the trail, offered their large affections to the efflorescence of the evening, their yearnings to the ripeness of spring.

Toad

Now turning the bend, we saw something odd, clearly out of place. Somewhere in the vast "rooms" of our species' brain, there's a Recognition Center alerting us to *novelty* which, like a surprise "Special News Bulletin" interrupting soothing music, arouses our curiousity. This object was essentially white, a little less than a foot in length and surprisingly straight. As we got closer, curiosity modulated into confoundedness. Again, nothing that I know of in nature is so smooth, so white, so precisely linear.

As you may have guessed, the "mystery object" was a creamy white *plastic straw* that had been thoughtlessly tossed into a wetland. My wife Pat fished it out. It was mostly white but it also had a thin red stripe down one side and a yellow one down the other. Some of the plastic had been chewed off and then disgarded. "Not for me" some critter must have thought to himself.

Nor for us either, this artifact from the world of fast foods, this "offspring" of chemical engineers, oil wells, tankers, pipelines, plastic extrusion processes, and robotic packing machines.

Oh, the delicacy of the day, its hushed, prayer-like moment — so rudely interrupted! And instantly, from eye to brain — feelings of disgust and anger — entered the "Judgmental Room" of my mind and then rippled down into my body. The effect? Briefly diminishing the color, the music, and dimming the wonder and sparkle of the moment.

Co-responsibility

Days later, I would reflect on that evening. I would wonder why I usually accept — with *little* thought or feeling — infinitely greater disfigurement of the natural world as I drive through our cities and suburbs. Or, for example, when I dispose of my own trash — week by week — each (plastic) bag destined for some "invisible" landfill.

I confess to living day-to-day mentally predisposed to a destructive state of denial, and also to a gross numbing of my native sensitivities, of accepting wide-ranging forms of social and environmental blight as "normal": light pollution, exhaust pollution, subtle chemical pollution, endless sprawl, and also of doing very little to prevent the cancers, the children's asthma, the mercury in fish, to name a few transgressions of my values, of my own covenant with our "rare Earth." And like the jewels of Indra's mythical net,

> *Jewels on Indra's net*
> *Reflect each other endlessly.*[21]

each of my actions (or inactions) *ripple out* into the universal realm: every choice, a microcosm reflecting throughout the macrocosm as in the ancient story of the mountain god, Indra:

> Indra is the god who lives on the top of mount Sumeru. In his heavenly palace is a huge net, every knot of which is adorned with a jewel...This image suggests the perfect interdependence in the whole universe...The net is woven of an infinite variety of brilliant gems, each with countless facets. Each gem reflects in itself every other gem.[22]

Alas, if I could only be more aware of what I am doing and what I am consuming, I would understand that *I too am co-responsible* for the poisons, for animal and plant extinctions, for global deforestation and our planet's slow but inexorable climate change.

> ...the most important precept of all is to live in awareness, to know what is going on, not only here, but there. For instance, when you eat a piece of bread, you may choose to be aware that our farmers, in growing the wheat, use chemical poisons a little too much. Eating the bread, we are somehow co-responsible for the destruction of our ecology.[23]

Let me briefly share with you a couple of illustrations from my own life. Lately, for example, I have been thinking about my driving habits: consider the fact that my wife and I drove to the nature trail! Each gallon of gasoline, when combined with atmospheric oxygen, adds some 19.694 pounds of carbon dioxide into the air.[24] Indeed, on a recent fill-up (a little more than a week of driving), I "consumed" 10.403 gallons of gas for 267.8 miles. That's 204 pounds of carbon dioxide originating from crude oil pumped from the earth, transported, refined, combusted, and finally released into the air. Furthermore, my own records indicate that I've averaged some 10,186 miles per year over the past four years (a little less than the U.S. average of 11,300 miles). And at 26 miles per gallon, that is 380 gallons of gasoline per year or almost 8000 pounds (4 tons) of carbon dioxide! My annual "carbon debt" seems to be, *not* a small jeweled reflection (of Indra's Net), but truly a sizable "*footprint*" launched into the atmosphere.

In addition, my driving has probably contributed something to urban ozone pollution close at hand, and also to acid rain that may well damage lakes and forests further away. In his book, *The Dying of the Trees*, Charles Little comments on the impact of mid-west industrial and transportation pollutants in killing off spruce groves in the Green Mountains of Vermont:

> The agents of their demise are invisible chemicals produced
> a thousand miles to the west without a by-your-leave or apol-
> ogy.[25]

Distant pollutants, writes Little, have literally altered the forest's soil structure and chemistry, leaching heavy metals into the topsoil. These red spruce stands, according to soil scientists, may *never* grow back.[26] From spruce forests to childhood asthma activated by urban ozone, to disastrous oil spills, to the tragic "9/11" attack and the continual chaos in the oil-rich Middle East, there's surely a vast array of transportation related "collateral damage" of my (our) excessive use of oil.[27]

Sometimes (in an economics class), when I complete my litany of social and environmental damages of my driving, students ask if I don't feel *guilty*. "I try not to" I say, because guilt usually dissipates over time, eventually to be replaced by a more comfortable state of *moral amnesia*.

Instead, I believe that the concept of co-responsibility should be seen as a healthy *tool for understanding*, a kind of force-field for Truth

— in the same spirit as other great religious insights such as Lao Tzu's, "So nourish the world, but do not control it, be in the world, but do not possess it,"[28] (from *Tao Te Ching*), or Jesus' puzzling "He that loveth his life shall lose it, he that will lose his life shall save it."[29] which was incidently one of poet Matthew Arnold's favorite meditations. "Such utterances," Arnold wrote, are not "stiff and stark external commands,"

> ...but things which have the most soul in them; because these can best sink down into our soul, work there, set up an influence, and form habits of conduct.[30]

So too the concept and commitment to personal and collective co-responsibility.

Global Capitalism

Another example (of many possibilities) from my own home-economy involved a purchase our family made years ago. In the summer of 1991 my wife and I put down new kitchen flooring. On the advice of our local building supply store, we dutifully bought the recommended underlayment: sheets of a thin, smooth, plywood called "lauan." Lauan is one of the varieties of Philippine mahogany of the genus *Shorea*. These four by eight foot panels originated from trees that can sometimes reach a height of 150 feet and a circumference of 85 feet or more![31]

I can easily visualize these ancient rainforests — from their underground roots to their overarching canopies — "cathedral" forests replete with unique, diverse, and fully functioning ecosystems including, of course, their wonderful groves of gentle behemoths, trees comparable in circumference to the great redwoods and sequoias of California. (It would take some 20 children to put their collective arms round a single trunk of the largest of these mahogany giants!) Such an image by itself should have given us pause in purchasing lauan mahogany for our kitchen subflooring.

Yet, imagine our shock and dismay when, a few months later, we discovered that the Philippine island of Leyte (a major source of lauan) had suffered massive flooding, death, and destruction traced to large-scale clear-cutting of Philippine mahogany removed from the island's mountainous slopes. With little foliage to break the energy of some six inches of rain (from tropical Hurricane Thelma), plus the absence of tree root systems that normally anchor the topsoil, an estimated 21 million cubic yards of earth washed down the mountain sides on November 5th 1991, creating a *ten foot* high wall of water, mud, and debris — all cascading into Leyte's Anilao River valley — and then continued to rage through, and scour the heart of the island's largest city, Ormoc. By the end of that week, some 6,000 residents were dead, tens-of thousands were homeless, and millions of dollars worth of crops had been ruined. Two days after the flood, New York Times reporter Seth Mydans pieced together various on-the-site observations:[32]

> Residents of Ormoc said the floodwaters, preceded by a great roar, uprooted trees, flushed cars down the streets and ripped wooden houses from their foundations.

Why did it happen? When Lito Osmena, Governor of the nearby Philippine island of Cebu presented his theory, I wondered if *our* family too didn't play some small role in this tragedy:

> The forests are gone and I guess over-logging is one of the major causes...That area gets several typhoons a year but they never resulted in something like this, and I think it is because the forests are gone...
> Illegal logging, with the complicity of local politicians and military oficiers, has recently become recognized as a major environmental problem in the Philippines. Forest cover is being stripped from the hillsides and erosion is degrading the land.

After the great flood, eye-witnesses reported additional details of that horrific day:

> The captain of an inter-island vessel, Porfirio Labugnay, interviewed in Cebu, said: "I saw bodies and animals, cows, pigs, and household applicances floating in the

sea off Ormoc city."

"People were in a panic," said Demetria Go, a 48-year-old resident. "They were scampering into the streets. Some children climbed up trees yelling for help. People were screaming as they ran from their houses."

Like individual drops of rain (dollar by dollar by dollar), these monetary pulses when added up, swell into a powerful river — a great global force that's literally beyond any individual or group's control. Add in greed, poverty, and political corruption. Add in clear-cutting shrouded from view (sounds muffled by distance), and you have a confluence of events ripe for human and biological tragedy on a massive scale.

Leyte's 1991 flood was *not* an "Act of God," but truly an act of humans — consumers, loggers, sellers, politicians, plus all the persuasive advocates for "unregulated free trade." Indeed, after the tragedy of Leyte, I can understand for the first time what author Helena Norberg-Hodge meant when she wrote:

> The ever-expanding scope and scale of the global economy obscures the consequences of our actions: In effect, our arms have been so lengthened that we no longer see what our hands are doing. Our situation exacerbates and furthers our ignorance, preventing us from acting out of compassion and wisdom.[33]

Also after Leyte, I'm able to better comprehend what environmentalists mean by an *"ecological footprint,"* a concept (like co-responsibility) that forces me to recognize my social and environmental responsibilities *beyond* my own immediate visual space.[34] (My own "footprint," for example, can be defined as the approximate quantity of land I use for my housing, transportation, waste disposal, food, etc.) Rough calculations indicate that each North American uses between 11 and 13 acres of productive land to meet their material requirements,[35] while an average person in India uses approximately *one* acre. After Leyte, the environmentalists' observation

...if everyone on Earth had the same levels of consumption as North Americans, we would need three planets to satisfy our demand.[36]

seems not only is plausible but might well be a thought or image that we can "sink down into our soul" (as the poet said) " work there, set up an influence, and form habits of conduct."

A "For-Profit Culture"

In thinking about these issues, I often get depressed. I feel as if I were literally *submerged in an ocean of commercialism*, drowning in a For-Profit Culture. It's to my left, my right; it's above me and below me. The bottom line is, well, "The Bottom Line." It's in our language,[37] it's in our schooling philosophy ("to get a good job"), it's in nearly every media niche that is saturated with commercialized "entertainments" along with their day-time (and night-time) flood-tide of marketing messages. It's in the *hourly* report: Dow Jones Industrials "are up" (or "down"). It's in politics bought and sold, it's in retail stores that never close, it's in electronic Televangelist "churches" promoting *material* "prosperity." Indeed, it seems to be deeply imbedded in many of our work and family issues: stress, debt, overwork, road rage/desk rage, loss of free time, deterioration of community, teen-age self-image issues, eating disorders, and environmental alienation.[38]

More than likely *you* contribute to this pervasive Capitalist Culture and, no doubt, so do I. Recently I checked out our family's "social responsibility" mutual stock fund and discovered (to my dismay) that we have inadvertently invested in the world's largest fast-food company (remember the plastic straw?), a major transnational forest products corporation, and three of the world's most profitable consumer retailers.

Who, I wonder, is *not* contributing — in some way — to those powerful economic forces which seem to sadden the heart and wound the soul? Forces, like the great flood of Leyte, that diminish Creation, damage the beauty and diversity of Tao's "ten-thousand things," and that slowly degrade our precious rare-earth?

It is time, perhaps, to take a second look at our oft-praised economic arrangement, to explore terrain *beyond* capitalism's efficiencies and innovations, its muscular ability to marshal resources, and its unquestioned productive might — time perhaps to pause and ask a simple yet vital question: "why is market capitalism — all too often — so destructive too?"

禍莫大於不知足

咎莫大於欲得

— 道德経、46

"Great trouble comes from not knowing what is enough..."

Chapter III:
What's Wrong With Capitalism?

Great trouble comes
From not knowing what is enough.
Great conflict arises
From wanting too much.[39]

Lao Tzu (*Tao Te Ching*)

Despite its materialistic virtues, *something's* amiss in the Land of Capitalism. That something is a quality — or *force* — that all too often violates the natural laws that normally insure Life's beauty and balance, its health and long-term continuity.

To search for that undermining force, let us pretend for a moment that you could literally "pick up" **Market Capitalism** as if it were a flawed gemstone. Now place it in the palm of your hand and turn it over and over, inspect it for defects, fissures, and possible flaws. Briefly, what would be the *economist's* perspective? Now angle it slightly differently: what would be the viewpoint of an *ecologist*? And finally, is it possible to look at our economy from a *prairie's* perspective, or that of an *old growth forest*?

Economist's Perspective

Economists *do* acknowledge capitalism's imperfections, often describing its defects as "market failures." These include the many unintended impacts ballooning beyond regular business costs into what economist's call "*externalities*," where consumption and profit-making have "spill-over effects" that all too often damage human health and landscapes, degrade water and air quality, endanger plant and animal species and possibly, over time, even alter the very stability of Earth's climate. And the remedy?

27

Corrective measures usually require government intervention: first to scientifically verify damages, then to initiate policies. These policies could include a "health tax" (on cigarettes), or a "green-tax" (on emissions), or the trading of pollution-credits, or enforcement of clean air, water, and endangered species laws, or the negotiation of global agreements (e.g. whaling, cloroflorocarbons, carbon dioxide, etc.) enforced by protocols, regulatory oversight, and international law.

Conceptually, these measures can be understood as a way to *motivate businesses and consumers to pay the full direct and indirect costs* ("full-cost accounting") of their economic activity, including the costs of collateral damages to natural and human environments. Simply put, *it's a fairness issue*, of playing the "game" (the "Capitalist Game") fair and square. Let us look at a contemporary illustration regarding human health, a concern recently brought to my attention by the Physicians for Social Responsibility, an environmental health advocacy group in Washington D.C.[40]

Childhood Asthma

The issue is the ever-worsening problem of childhood asthma. Indeed, there's good evidence that asthma is exacerbated by truck and automobile pollution, including elevated ground-level ozone in U.S. cities. A *U.S. News and World Report* article on the subject of transportation gridlock and urban sprawl noted:

> During the 1996 Olympics, Atlanta officials took dramatic steps to limit car traffic in the city. The measures work so well the number of cars in the morning rush hour dropped by 22.5 percent. But there was another benefit: The number of children suffering asthma attacks, a leading cause of childhood illness, dropped dramatically.[41]

Atlanta's inadvertent "experiment" and its intriguing results dovetail with other studies suggesting that ozone increases the incidence of asthmatic attacks (especially for inner-city children).[42]

Armed with this information, I recently approached a state lawmaker asking if he would consider proposing a modest increase in our state's gas tax (say, ½ cent) earmarked, not for the usual highway construction and maintenance, but to reimburse parents for asthma related expenses. I told him that "I was upset because I was paying *too little* for my gas," disturbed that I was "not paying my fair share of the spill-over effects of my driving." I asked why we should force families with sick children to subsidize an artificially low-cost transportation system? Relevant expenses might include:

*emergency trips to the hospital
*wages lost attending sick children
*asthma medication, inhalers, charcoal-impregnated
  face masks[43]
*doctors fees and higher insurance premiums

Drivers, I said, should also be responsible for the extra costs of rescheduling outdoor sporting events, since many of these children are forced to remain indoors during periodic ozone alerts. An increase in our federal and/or state gasoline tax would be a good beginning, a step toward the economist's ideal of "full-cost accounting."

Increasing gas taxes would not only help pay legitimate health costs, it would also give a small nudge to many of us to drive *slightly* less often. In addition, it would motivate *some* drivers to purchase a more fuel-efficient vehicle the next time they were in the market including "hybrids" (gasoline + electric), and perhaps eventually, fuel-cell cars powered by clean-burning hydrogen. Ultra small changes in our driving habits — multiplied by millions and millions of drivers — will eventually make a small but positive difference in air quality. And if drivers were actually paying all of their spill-over costs,[44] they would have a financial incentive to do more walking or perhaps more biking. Studies show that, surprisingly, a quarter of trips are *less than one mile*, and fourteen percent are less than half-mile![45]

Both walkers and bikers in some cities have already pressured governments to promote more walkable and bike friendly neighborhoods. Whereas Atlanta is infamous for its *un*walkability, Portland Oregon has some sixteen "Pedestrian Districts" where the street-design, sidewalks, and traffic laws give pedestrians priority.[46] And in Davis California, there are safe, dedicated bike-lanes on most city streets. Moreover, developers in Davis are required to provide bike access to new residential and commercial developments.

Full-cost accounting would also encourage more carpooling and, if available, greater use of public transit. Not only would urban adults and children breathe easier, but trees and wildlife would benefit too. And finally, if truckers and car owners paid their full direct and indirect costs, economists believe it would begin to reduce road congestion while diminishing the political pressure to widen roads and highways and thus minimize damage to local communities and to the landscape itself.

Next time you happen to be stalled in a traffic jam (perhaps on a hot day, tempers building, distant buildings smog-obscured), take a moment to "think like an economist" — i.e. *to see the road as an amenity with high demand combined with relatively low costs.* Authors Terry More and Paul Thorsnes[47] comment that traffic gridlock can best be understood with an analogy: imagine you are constructing an outdoor concert arena that would host only the most popular music groups. Assume too, that you plan to subsidize each of the concerts meaning that the tickets (like the daily use of roads) are free! How large would you build the arena? As long as concerts are subsidized, it would be difficult to build one large enough. You may even discover that no matter how much you expand capacity, the arena will never, for all practical purposes, be big enough to satisfy projected demand. Gridlock![48] (Sound familiar?)

Of course the economist's perspective — even with good science, logic, and sensible remedies on its side — is usually no match for well-funded special interests. In the case of increasing gas taxes for legitimate spill-over costs, the powerful highway, oil, and automobile lobbies will often block legislation that would, (as they see it), "harm" their industries. Indeed, in response to my gas tax suggestion, my representative told me, "I understand your point and, yes, I even agree with you," but then added: "Jim, you'd better forget it, politically it ain't going to happen."

Ecologist's Perspective

I dream of a day when among others, parents, children, politicians, economists, CEOs, bankers, miners, loggers, etc., make decisions based upon a genuine ecological consciousness, including an understanding and full appreciation of the *broad spectrum of environmental values* that allow ecosystems to be healthy and whole.

As an example, consider once more an old growth forest, such as the few that still exist in the United States, or the mountainous mahogany groves of Leyte, Philippines, discussed earlier. In what ways would the ecologist's perspective differ from that of a for-profit capitalist? To answer this question, I find it helpful to picture in my mind an image of a playground Teeter-Totter that has a large, colorful basket at each end. The basket on the left side is marked CAPITALIST VALUES and the one on the right, ECOLOGICAL VALUES. Next, children at each end begin placing weighted objects into the baskets representing the two different sets of values. What "weights" would they put into the CAPITALIST basket? Benefits might include:

* the monetary value of wood products (including export earnings)
* incomes for loggers, truckers, and saw-mill operators
* increased sales for equipment, including manufacturing jobs
* an increase in the company's short-term profits
* corporate stock price would go up adding value to stockholder portfolios

Importantly, from the "for-profit" point of view, there would be pressure to maximize these values in the short run by clear-cutting the forest.

Now turning our attention to the right side ("ecological values"), what representative "weights" would the children put into this basket? In some old growth forests (such as the Menominee Indian Reservation in Wisconsin) logging provides modest *economic* benefits and the tribe has been able to maintain the forest's original ecological make-up for generations. The Menominee remove a relatively small portion of the forest each year using a concept of "sustainable yield management principles"[49] that incorporates *selective cutting based on cultural constraints* laid down by the tribal elders over a hundred years ago. With a selective cutting strategy, there is some monetary value in lumber, logging, and saw mill operator's jobs, and *some* export profits. But the return in the short-run is lower (compared to clear-cutting), yet over many many years, incomes are relatively stable.[50]

Now in addition to the modest economic benefits, let's ask the children to put into their basket the following "weights, " representing a broader spectrum of ecological, scientific, and spiritual values:
* a habitat for endangered plants and animals
* the possibility of discovering new and effective "wonder drugs"
* low-cost recreation plus a "living classroom" to study a healthy ecosystem
* a source of beauty, inspiration, and spiritual sustenance[51]
* the innate capacity to reduce erosion and soil loss and to recharge aquifers
* cooler, cleaner, and healthier streams and rivers (compared to a clear-cut forest)
* the recycling of nutrients and the production of new top-soil
* the ability to sequester atmospheric carbon and generate oxygen
* the stabilization of weather and climatic patterns

Tropical forests may also produce a sustainable supply of nuts, berries, valuable barks, tubers, mushrooms, medicines,[52] etc. for those who know how to find them and, in the case of Leyte, Philippines, a commitment to ecological sound selective cutting may have prevented the tragic flooding that killed over 6,000 people in 1991. From an ecological perspective, forests literally *roll up their sleeves and "work hard"* to provide invisible, yet important benefits, a myriad of so-called "ecological services"[53] based on the productivity of the forest's intrinsic natural capital. In comparison, the children's ecological-values basket ought to *easily outweigh* the capitalist basket. Yet in our current global economic arrangement, ultra powerful forces of corrupt politicians, obsessions with "unfettered" free trade—plus, of course inflated greed, short-run profit maximization (and an ignorance of ecological values) we find that the capitalist basket usually wins out. It's as if the global economy were (metaphorically) "defying gravity" as well as other essential laws of the natural world.

A Prairie's Perspective (and The Future of Capitalism)

If I were asked to pick an analogy from which I might learn the principles for a future, balanced, capitalism, some would think my example a little odd: my choice would be a native prairie ecosystem I walk through nearly every day. It's not exactly global "free-market" capitalism, but like a pristine rain-forest, this prairie is a living example of what might be called *local natural capitalism.*

Big Blue Stems

Indeed, my prairie has become a mentor for me—as if it were trying to teach its lessons to a slow-learning, yet earnest economics student.[54]   I have discovered that this flowering grassland is not only attractive, but exceptionally diverse and, like a model sustainable economy, remarkably productive—turning sunbeams into biotic beauty and eventually converting vegetation into rich, deep, loamy soils.

In addition, this prairie ecosystem has achieved something quite amazing: *an exquisite balance between life and death* — humming along year after year in a kind of steady-state, economic efficiency. It recycles virtually everything and unfailingly, it blooms anew — spring after spring and every summer too!

Prairies are resilient in severe drought; yet they can also handle a week of drenching rain. Mole, Monarch, and Meadowlark survive there. Blue stems and Indian grasses live in prairies too, and so do Black-Eyed-Susans, Purple Prairie Clovers, Stiff Goldenrods, and late-summer blooms of Blazing Stars.

Sometimes I enjoy laying down in the prairie, *accepting gravity* as it were, my back stretched out along the rough ground, my eyes taking in sun, cloud, flower, seedpod, and there "high" above me, tufts of grasses bending down and up, up and down as if there was an invisible ocean of wind blown waves. Likewise, according to ecologist David Abram, our own technological civilization also must (someday)

> accept the invitation of gravity and settle back into the land,
> its political and economic structures diversifying into the var-
> ied contours and rhythms of a more-than-human earth.[55]

So one might ask: "what direction, what trajectory will we be able to follow to a more natural, indeed a more *balanced* capitalism? Can our economy readjust and redress its spill-over effects and correct its corrosive *externalities*? Can we conserve (as if an ecological consciousness were our "second nature") our planet's grasslands, soils, ancient forests, subterranean waters, its rivers and reefs? Like the prairie, can we find a more harmonic, natural equilibrium that abounds in beauty, balance, and biodiversity? And finally, can we utilize energies renewable, make consumables durable (and fully recyclable) while preserving Earth's realms of amazement, its landscapes of surprise?

Harmony & Balance

Of course these principles of harmony and balance — _individually and collectively_ — are not new. Over two-thousand years ago they became the foundation of an emerging Taoist philosophy in China and later became incorporated in a "cultural treasure" and popular Chinese martial art called "t'ai chi ch'uan." Let's now take a closer look.

Part II
Balance and Rebirth

故有無相生、難易相成

長短相較、高下相傾

音声相和、

— 道德経、2

"Difficult and easy balance each other..."

Chapte IV
Taoism and the Principle of Balance

Difficult and easy balance each other.
Long and short complete one another.
High and low rely on each other.
Pitch and tone make harmony together.

Lao Tzu[56]

Tilting my head, cupping my ear, I sometimes wish I could hear the voice of the Taoist poet/philosopher, Lao Tzu of 2400 years ago. Indeed, if he were to suddenly step into our world, what would interest him? What, I wonder, would the Old Sage say?

If I understand Taoist thought correctly, Lao Tzu would be curious about our life-styles but probably conclude (as noted in the previous chapter) that contemporary Western culture is deeply, disturbingly out of balance. Like the children's teeter-totter or perhaps like a dangerously misshapen, ever-wobbly wheel, our work habits, our business practices, our entertainments, our day-to-day preoccupations tend to be *overweighted* in so-called "*yang*" forces.

On the individual level, it is as if we lived (to use a modern-day metaphor) inside a pressurized, linear cyclotron of high energy physics. For too many of us, it is life literally in bondage to time-dictated, staccato-like activities, where families are literally swept along, full-throttle, in day-to-day fragmented experiences, and where working/living environments suffer from excessive brightness, loudness, glare and glitter.

天下莫柔於水而功堅者

莫之能勝 其無以易之

弱之勝強 柔之勝剛

天下莫不知 莫能行

—道德経·78

"Nothing under heaven is more pliable than water..."

Yin/Yang Balance

Although the *yang* qualities of energy and ambition can be healthy (in moderation), according to Taoism, *not* when starved for counterbalancing *yin* qualities: the soft, the intuitive, the conservative; of quiet moments of equilibrium and inner peace.

In Taoist landscape paintings, *yang* is frequently symbolized by a mountain whereas *yin* is the valley with its ever-flowing river. *Yin* is humble — yet powerful too!

> *Nothing under heaven is more pliable than water*
> *But when amassed, there is nothing on Earth*
> *That can withstand its force.*
> *That the soft overcomes the hard*
> *And the yielding conquers the strong*
> *Is a fact known to all men yet utilized by none.*[57]

Yin can also be understood as the principle of the "female," the ecological, of Earth itself. If *yin* is invisible and fecund, *yang* is energized and ambitious. Again, *yang* requires the essential qualities of *yin*. Likewise, *yin* needs the counterbalancing of *yang*. Neither is better as *both* are complementary and necessary to the whole: "Mountains and Waters are a dyad" the poet wrote,

"...that together makes wholeness possible."[58]

And like most spiritual traditions, Taoism also has its essential symbols for reminding and reinforcing these key principles. Perhaps the most important symbol (indeed, the most recognizable) is the familiar T'ai Chi Circle (or *yin/yang* diagram).

T'ai Chi Circle

Its meaning? Huston Smith, in his book, *The World's Religions,* comments that the black (*yang*) and white (*yin*) polaritity,

> ..sums up all of life's basic oppositions: good/evil, active/passive, positive/negative, light/dark, summer/winter, male/female. But though the halves are in tension, they are not flatly opposed; they complement and balance each other. Each invades the other's hemisphere and takes up its abode in the deepest recess of its partner's domain. And in the end both find themselves resolved by the circle that surrounds them, the *Tao* in all its eternal wholeness.[59]

T'ai chi literally means the principle of *yin/yang* balance.[60] According to Chinese philosophy it can also be symbolized by the "ridge pole" of a house. Take a moment to picture in your mind a simple dwelling and its uppermost horizontal beam running east and west, that is, the point where the south-facing section of the roof (sunny/warm/*yang*) joins with the north facing side (shaded/cool/*yin*). Along this "stillpoint" two opposites are joined together.

Likewise, t'ai chi balance can be represented by the *ridge of a hill.* In climbing the hill, for example, one can *physically experience* the essential *yin and yang* qualities as represented by the dark and light sides of the hill respectively.[61]

Barn Bluff, Redwing, Minnesota

Barn Bluff

Not too long ago my wife Pat and I spent the morning working our way up a large bluff overlooking the Mississippi. We began our ascent on the shady (*yin*) side, immediately entering a dark, maple/basswood/birch woodland. As our eyes adjusted to the relative darkness, our skin began to sense the shady path's moist atmosphere. Here and there we encountered springs of clear, cool water creating pockets of chilled air. A "hush" was felt. The mood of was of receiving...yielding.

Biologically *yin* is a world of earthworms, liverworts, horsetails, and low, lovely Lady and Maidenhair ferns. *Yin* is the quality of *snailness*. The small, white snail shells — contrasting dramatically against the dark soil — were everywhere (here and there I bent down with a hand lens magnifying their magnificent spirals). We also saw deep-green mosses clothing small pieces of broken bedrock, while above us, we noted dark openings of cave entryways in the upper layers of the limestone. It is as if we had entered an ancient world of Earth's primal beginnings, of Taoism's "Mystical Womb," Lao Tzu's

...darkness within darkness.[62]

Rounding the bluff, we begin walking in a more southerly direction, entering what felt like a "wall" of sunbeams. Our eyes were forced to adjust to a new, bright *yang* world. (An old "reptilian" part of me responded to the deep pleasure of the sun's radiant warmth). Our visual depth-of-field increased as the eyes adjusted to the brighter scene now layered with greater energies and dimensions of color and space. Before us was a classic "Goat Prairie." Far from *yin*'s ferns, snails, and mosses, on the sun-warmed *yang* side, we were suddenly dazzled by the blues of Blazing Stars, the purples of Leadplant, the yellows of Sunflowers and Goldenrod, and the bright ruby reds of Staghorn Sumac. Here, too, were bumblebees and wasps full of wild buzzings and fantastic zipabouts and too, dozens of Monarchs flapping and gliding their bright orange wings in and about the flowering prairie grassland in front of us. If t'ai chi balance is represented by the ridgepole of a house, it's also on the ridge-line of this bluff some 334 feet above the Mississippi River. To our left (north), the shadowy *yin* side and beyond, the great river valley. And to our right, bright *yang* colors of the prairie and beyond that, the busy, bustling city of Red Wing, Minnesota.

T'ai Chi Ch'uan

At the individual level, this balance can actually be *experienced* in the practice of the gentle martial art called t'ai chi ch'uan.[63] Benefits include the "gift of balance,"[64] in the form of greater physical stability (fewer falls, especially for the elderly), and also the balancing of one's ch'i (*qi*) or intrinsic life energies. In addition, t'ai chi has been known to improve blood circulation and enhance joint flexibility. And as an individual antidote to our high-pressured life-styles, t'ai chi ch'uan, in its slow-motioned choreographed "meditation in movement," has been said to effectively lower stress.[65] Practitioners often report moments of *mindfulness*, of inner-peace and respite from the preoccupations, fears, and the cacophonous "thought-noise" of the mind. As one t'ai chi teacher put it,

> Our minds are so full of inner dialogue, so busy with plan-
> ning, remembering, analyzing, blaming, or explaining, that
> we rarely come to this quiet but present state of mind.[66]

Mindfulness, or "keeping one's consciousness alive to the present reality,"[67] implies an ongoing awareness of breath, body, and also
of one's immediate natural surroundings: ground, atmosphere, gravity,
of nature itself. Indeed, across t'ai chi ch'uan's history, it's the *natural*
metaphors that have stuck in describing many of the "postures" or
movements. The feet, for example, should be "rooted like a pine
tree;"[68] whereas the upper body becomes as fluid "as a cloud or river."
T'ai chi teacher and writer Bob Klein describes his experience as a kind
of *natural awakening*, as it were, where the world "comes alive..."

> You are now perceiving the world without the intermediary
> of mind. This is direct perception.[69]

It's as if we were capable of activating an ancestral or "species
memory," of returning to an earlier, pre-human, condition—back, back
to our animal origins, recognizing (as Klein puts it) "signposts written
in some long-forgotten language"[70] and rediscovering "the power and
gracefulness of the creatures of nature that exist potentially within each
of us."[71]

For example, one early precursor to modern t'ai chi ch'uan was
an exercise called "The Five Animal Frolics," known for its imitation
of the crane (for the quality of relaxation), the bear (for strength), the
monkey (for flexibility), the deer (for grace), and finally, the tiger (for
power).[72]

Approximately seven hundred years ago a Taoist monk —
Chang San-feng — "discovered" t'ai chi ch'uan's essential principles
in a dream sequence featuring a snake and a crane. In his dream he witnessed what seemed like an epic contest. Normally, of course, the
snake would be in grave danger from the crane's dagger-like beak; yet
in the dream, Snake was remarkably skilled in *evading* each and every
attack. His "victory" was not from his fierceness or explosive power,

but because of a quality of heightened sensitivity combined with precision timing and *yielding* when necessary. Later, Chang actually witnessed these same two play out their battle in a recapitulation of his dream.[73] At that moment (legend has it), the so-called "Soft Internal School" of martial arts was born.[74]

In observing someone practicing the t'ai chi ch'aun exercise, it is difficult to actually "see" the animal postures because of its slow ("loris-paced") moves. Yet they're there. Examples include: crane (*"White Crane Spreads Her Wings"*), tiger (*"Embrace Tiger, Return to Mountain"*), monkey (*"Repulse Monkey"*), rooster (*"Golden Rooster Stands on One Leg"*), and snake (*"Snake Creeps Down"*). Other postures include references to natural phenomena such as clouds (*"Cloudy Hands"*) and a well known night-sky constellation (*"Stepping Up to the Stars of the Big Dipper"*).

C'hi ("*qi*")

Ch'i

In physics, when an electron receives energy from the outside, it is capable of expanding into a larger orbit.[75] Likewise, according to Chinese traditional medicine, t'ai chi students who can utilize the ch'i or *qi*[76] can also gain additional energy from their environment. Author and teacher Ken Cohen explains:

> We live in a field of qi, "vital breath' or "life energy." Yet, like a fish in water or a bird in flight, we are unaware of the medium that supports us. Qigong means "working with the qi." It is the ancient Chinese art and science of becoming aware of this life energy and learning how to control its flow through the precise choreography of posture, movement, Respiratory technique, and meditation.[77]

And like an electron absorbing energy and expanding into a wider orbit, practitioners can, (according to Cohen), experience a greater awareness or *expansiveness* with the natural world:

> Expansiveness means that your body feels open and expansive, Without constriction or hindrance..[it's] the subjective feeling of blending into the environment. Your feet reach through the ground into the earth. Your head joins with the sky, your skin with qi.[78]

Similarly, Lao Tzu commented in *The Tao Te Ching* that "the way to the Tao" is through cultivating tranquility and softening, so that "the inside self becomes the outside world."[79]

The natural world may now seem "friendlier" as you experience a greater sense of "kinship" with the birds, the trees, the river, the little animals coming and going[80] — the same quality perhaps that Taoist landscape artists felt as they composed their paintings of mountains, clouds, valleys, rivers, insects, birds, while depicting man's relatively insignificant place in the cosmological scheme of things.

道生一、一生二、二生三、

三生萬物。萬物負陰

而抱陽，沖氣以為和

　　——道德經、42

"Tao produced the One..."

Chinese Cosmology

In addition to a health exercise, t'ai chi ch'uan is also a ritual re-enactment of Chinese _cosmology_ — i.e., the cyclical rebirth and evolution of the universe.[81] Initiated by the Great Ancestor (Tao), the sequence of events are outlined in chapter 42 of the _Tao Te Ching_:

> _Tao produced the One_
> _The One produce the Two._
> _The Two produced the three_
> _And the Three produced the ten-thousand things._[82]

When, for example, you stand in the "Beginning" posture, you are at the stage of "the One" (see above), or what the Chinese call _Wu Chi_. _Wu Chi_ is simply "The Great Void." Although a void, _Wu Chi_ also has _infinite creative potential_, replete with probabilities and possibilities — a "fertile emptiness"[83] if you will.

Wu Chi Circle

Sometimes I enjoy closing my eyes, breathing in while picturing an artist dipping her brush into black ink and, with a singular mind and a steady hand, drawing a beautiful empty circle — the circle of *Wu Chi*. It is empty, yes, but like a bellows, *Wu Chi* is capable of producing "breath at will."[84] Eyes still closed, I exhale and see a gentle expansion of the *Wu Chi* circle — a bulge of *yang* energy. Likewise, with an in-breath, the principle of *yin* is born.

To summarize, the "One" (*Wu Chi*) with the assistance of Breath, produces "the "Two" (*yin/yang* or the "marriage" of Heaven and Earth). And then like a mother and a father giving birth to a child, the "Two" produces the "Three" or the familiar T'ai Chi Circle (*yin/ yang* diagram). And finally, once a mutual, dynamic interactive *yin/ yang* balance is achieved, creative evolution takes place in the rebirth of the Universe:

"And the Three produced the ten-thousand things"

At the stage of "three," one might say that there's no longer a "Creator," *only creativity*.[85] And as stressed earlier, it is the *dynamic balance* that's so critical to maintaining a healthy state of creativity and diversity. In a memorable ecological illustration, author Diane Dreher brings home this point. Consider, for example, a tidal pool on the edge of the ocean:

> Every day the tide washes in with new sources of water and nutrients, providing the active force of *yang*. The *yin* enclosure in the rocky Cliffs protects the tiny world from the pounding waves. Balance is vital. Pools too far from the rushing water become stagnant, excessively *yin*. Too close to the *yang* of the turbulent surf, other pools hold only sand and water, too unsettled to sustain life. Nature renews itself by balancing these forces.[86]

And also...don't the buds of fruit trees require a *yin* period of cold dormancy to become fruit in the warm (*yang*) months of the summer? Our own *yin* "dormancy" might, in turn, take the form of quiescent periods — prayer, meditation, yoga — of momentarily stopping "our thinking and habit energies."[87] T'ai chi ch'uan can be helpful in the same way, where one can — according to *qigong* teacher Ken Cohen — literally experience

> stillness within activity—the body is moving, but the mind is clear, still, and undisturbed.[88]

Yang T'ai Chi Short Form

If you are now so inclined, perhaps you would like to take a few moments to try doing a little t'ai chi. Out of the thirty-seven movements of the Yang family short form, let us try both the "Beginning" posture and "Ward-Off Left" as popularized by the late t'ai chi Master Cheng Man-ch'ing (1901-1975).[89]

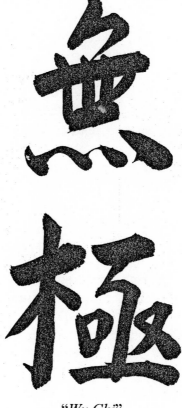

"Wu Chi"

It's best to be outdoors, surrounded by nature — i.e., in a park, a woodland, near a river, or simply in a back yard (preferably near trees). Next, face north. Now take a moment to place your feet *parallel to each other* and roughly shoulder-length apart. Bend your knees slightly. Very importantly — can you relax? Can you allow gravity to help "settle" your body into position? The Chinese word for "relaxation" is *song* (pronounced "shoong") implying a *conscious loose/limberness* (without tension, yet without any hint of collapsing). Pay special attention to relaxing the neck, shoulders, chest, wrists and hands.

Again, you should feel your body's weight sinking down, down, as if "rooted like pine tree." T'ai chi writer and teacher Linda Lehrhaupt once observed her two-year-old daughter, Taya, standing *as if perfectly rooted*, like a true t'ai chi ch'uan Master (helped, Linda noted, by a gravitational "pull" inside Taya's diapers).[90] In turn, Mom used a mental picture of herself wearing a diaper "full of stones" to gain the sensation of "heavy," relaxed rootedness.

Our family is also fortunate to live with a "Master" of gravity: our female cat "Buddy." Have you ever tried to move a *totally relaxed* cat off the table? Even on a glossy surface, it's surprisingly difficult. If I try to move her, I always underestimate the amount of force required. If I think, "I ought to be able to move her with one unit of push-power, it usually takes more like four units to get results. (Perfect *song*!)

Next, place your hands down next to your thighs, palms facing backward. Take a few moments and imagine your are literally "resting in *Wu Chi*." In addition, the quality of your breath should be "fine, long, calm, and slow."[91] Your breath should feel as if it is rising, not from the chest area, but from the center of gravity, an area perhaps an inch or two below your navel. Babies, of course, are natural abdominal breathers and it is recommended that t'ai chi students do the same.

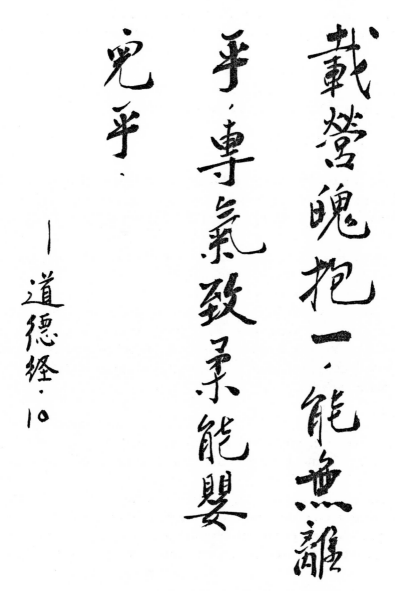

載營魄抱一能無離
乎，專氣致柔能嬰
兒乎。

——道德經·10

"Can you keep the spirit..."

Lao Tzu made the same point when he asked,

>*Can you keep the spirit and body without scattering,*
>*Can you concentrate your mind to use breath,*
>*Making it soft and quiet as an infant's?*[92]

From *Wu Chi*'s quiet attentiveness, begin to *raise* your arms in front of your body making sure that there is no tension in the wrists (i.e., let your fingers droop slightly). Breathe *in* as your arms rise. (Here you can picture your arms "floating up" as if they were rising up in salt-water.)

When your arms reach the upper chest level, slowly breath *out* and at the same time, gently straighten your fingers. Pretend that your hands and fingers were filling with the "life energy" rising from your center of gravity. (I personally find it helpful to imagine my fingers to be *like fresh new leaves in springtime*, sensitively exploring their environment as they slowly expand outward.)

Now, withdraw your arms inward toward the chest while simultaneously relaxing your wrists. As your hands approach the chest, lower your arms back down to your sides. (With loose wrists, your fingers should feel like soft, pliable "seaweed" being pulled gracefully back down, down, into the "water.")

At this point, t'ai chi's *Beginning* posture modulates into the next movement as you put more and more of your body weight into your *left* leg. Imagine this leg as a "hollow pillar" *filling with gravity*.

Now with all your "*yang*" weight in the left foot, turn slightly to the right (east). As the waist turns, the right foot (fully "*yin*" relaxed), should automatically turn to the east also. Meanwhile, your hands slowly align themselves as if they were holding an imaginary beach ball, left arm/hand on the bottom, right arm/hand rounded on top of the ball's imaginary circumference. Now without stopping, transfer your weight into the *right* foot. Check to make sure that your body is fully upright and relaxed. (Eyes too should have a relaxed *song* quality, of gazing "inward," with soft, unfocused eyes.)

Next, *glide* your body to the east while at the same time, *lowering your awareness* as much as possible Think earthworm! — that is your "attentiveness" makes its way, slowly, confidently though the subsoil. As you move, it is now the right leg that "fills" with gravity. If that analogy is too abstract, imagine the leg becoming filled-up with free-flowing *mud* — as if it is becoming a part of the ground itself!

"Ward-off left"

With all your weight in the right leg, turn slightly to the left while taking a step (to the north) with the (unweighted) left leg. Again check to see that you have approximately a shoulder's width distance between your feet. Your right hand now moves to the lower right hip area (palm down) and your left hand moves upward to the front. (Your two hands pass each other as if they were "pulling taffy.") At the end of this posture–called *Ward Off Left* —the left hand/arm should end up in a gently curved horizontal position with your palm facing your upper chest. Good!

Balance

If you can do these two movements — perhaps feeling a little *less* stressed and a little *more* centered, if you perhaps feel a little calmer, sensing that quality of *expansiveness*:

> *Mind is calm:*
> *rocks and trees*
> *much better...*[93]

then you've sampled the wonderful sensation of t'ai chi balance that's self-contained in this gentle martial art. Indeed, you may want take time to learn more about t'ai chi's history, philosophy and practice with a teacher, a workshop or perhaps explore some of the videos and books available on the subject.[94]

In addition, you'll have experienced the beginning of the Taoist version of "the dance of cosmology," originating at the headwaters of creation (*Wu Chi*) then modulating into a dynamic *yin/yang* balance (and its infinite creative possibilities)—a rebirth giving rise to the "ten-thousand things" and on to the evolution of the Universe itself!

Chapter V
T'ai Chi and the Ten-Thousand Things

I am satisfied with the mystery of the eternity of life and with the awareness and a glimpse of the marvelous structure of the existing world...

[The scientist's] religious feeling takes the form of a rapturous amazement at the harmony of natural law...

How can cosmic religious feeling be communicated from one person to another? In my view, it is the most important function of art and science to awaken this feeling and keep it alive in those who are receptive to it.

Albert Einstein[95]

Playfully, let's take a moment and ask: "If the *art* of t'ai chi symbolically recapitulates the evolution of the Universe (the "ten-thousand things"), how might t'ai chi's movements relate to the unfolding of the cosmos as seen from the instruments, discoveries, and understandings of modern *science*?

For example, assuming *Wu Chi* represents essential *nothingness* (the "Great Void") before the Big Bang, then the "Beginning" movement (as described in the previous chapter) would correlate with the Big Bang itself some thirteen to fourteen billion years ago — that is, the beginning of space, time, gravity, and matter.

Cosmic Inflation

Then, within the first trillion-trillion-trillionths of a second,[96] the Universe's stupendous spark of creativity swelled up, like a hyper-inflated sphere — from a size a billion times smaller than a proton to somewhere between the size of a marble and the size of a beach-ball.[97] Recall that in the *Ward Off Left* posture, you "hold" an imaginary ball of ch'i (left hand on the bottom, right hand on the top). Thus if you had (magically) been transported back to the beginning of time, and happened to witness the birth of the Universe, you could literally hold the Universe's cosmic everything between the palms of your hands!

Then, after this first fraction of a fraction of a second, the Big Bang's expansion settled into a comparatively leisurely pace, inviting forth an unfurling — like the frond of a fern — the Universe's unique personality as it refashioned the energies, particles, chemistries, and the universal rhythms into the everyday Cosmos as we know it.

Rhythms

Moving along in the t'ai chi form, I too note various rhythms within and without. For example, one *weighted* leg gently modulates into an *unweighted* leg (*yang* to *yin*). The body too assumes first, a contracting posture (*yin*), then an expansive posture (*yang*). Contraction...expansion. In addition, one's breath adds an additional rhythm: inhaling and exhaling, again and again.

T'ai chi author and teacher, Waysun Liao, advises his readers to feel, if they can, their internal energies as the "rhythmic power waves of the universe;"[98] similarly, another t'ai chi teacher writes that each movement can be understood as the rhythm of Tao itself, "the baseline rhythm present in the midst of all the other rhythms in the universe."[99] From the perspective of (scientific) cosmology, what was that primal "baseline rhythm" of the infant Universe? Was it perhaps a form of "music?" I was surprised to learn that astronomers now have evidence that early on, the Universe literally "rang like a bell," where (gravitational) high-pressure areas interacted with (radiation-induced) low-pressure areas *to make sound*. Again, if you had been able to witness that particular moment (something less than 300,000 years after the Big Bang), you might have heard a form of music! Science writer Ron Cowen, in his article "Sounds of the Universe Confirm Big Bang," comments on this surprising discovery:

> Whenever gravity caused matter to compress, the pressure exerted by the trapped photons offered resistence. The tug-of-war between gravity and radiation pressure generated acoustic oscillations, which are regions of higher and lower pressure *that have the same form of sound waves*.[100]

Thus, from original "chaos" comes the beginnings of "cosmos," an identifiable order and harmony plus (as its companion word *cos-*

metics suggests) an emerging embryonic *beauty* that will eventually form structures of stars, galaxies and clusters of galaxies. (I will pretend for a moment that these early density fluctuations, or ripples "wrinkled in the fabric of space-time"[101] are the equivalent of the *Tao Te Ching*'s metaphorical "Mother" or "Great Ancestor" — "Like an ancestor/ From which all things come...Whose offspring it may be/ I do not know."[102])

My movements now glide through *Lift Hands, Shoulder Strike, White Crane Spreads its Wing,* and *Brush Left Knee*, as well as a "strumming-like" posture called *Play the P'i P'a* (a Chinese musical instrument similar to the lute). Furthermore, in each of these early postures, I become more and more aware of the movement's subtle contraction and expansion phases: contraction and expansion, again and again.

Stellar Contractions & Expansions

Consider now the early universe's contraction of nebular dust condensing, over time, into stars. Later, these stars gently expanded either into a "planetary nebula" or (depending on the size of the star), exploded into supernovas. And each cycle of stellar (birth) contractions and (death) expansions would give birth to new and more complex elements: hydrogen to helium, "cooked" and recycled again and again into carbon, oxygen, silicon, and iron, atoms of our minds and bodies, indeed, of Tao's "ten-thousand things."

On my wall are four telescopic photographs: the first is of a 1960's vintage Palomar Observatory photograph of the Pleiades star cluster in the constellation Taurus. Four-hundred light-years away, the Pleiades represents comparatively young stars having recently contracted into a beautiful open cluster of bright stars. (Promise yourself to check them out with a pair of binoculars some cold, crisp, winter night. These famous "Seven Sisters," shining with the brilliance of diamonds will make your heart dance.) Next to the Pleiades is a photograph of the Veil nebula, a supernova remnant fifteen hundred light years away. (Should one be so lucky to see the Veil some summer night, through a medium-sized telescope, it will appear as an arc-shaped filament of "cosmic tease" best encountered with slightly averted eyes.)

The Pleiades Cluster and Veil Nebula are examples of both stellar contractions and expansions thus representing the great primal rhythm of element-making. A third photograph (from the Hubble Space Telescope) is of Orion's Nebula's newly forming stars, while next to it is a picture of the "Crab" Nebula (in the constellation Taurus)—one more example of a supernova reminant.

As I glide through the middle of the Yang short form including *Retreating Monkey*, *Diagonal Flying*, and then a pleasurable side-to-side motion called *Cloudy Hands*, I think about *rain* and wonder, "where does water come from?"

Water's Origin

Apparently the origins of water also go back to early generations of stellar creation and destruction. Indeed, once oxygen atoms had been formed by the process of nuclear fusion, they combined with hydrogen to form water. For example, in Orion's "stellar nursery," not only are new stars forming, but the Nebula is currently creating huge quantities of water. Researchers estimate that every twenty-four minutes Orion produces enough water to fill virtually all of Earth oceans.[103] In addition to being the cosmic "elixir" of life, water is also important for the birth of Orion's baby stars:

> Such a cosmic gusher is a good thing for stars too, because they need a splash of water to radiate heat and keep their cool. A collapsing cloud of hydrogen heats up so quickly that it can blow apart before it forms.[104]

Eventually, some of the water took the form of comets. Then, approximately four billion years ago, Earth itself was bombarded by uncountable numbers of asteroids and comets offering, as it were, free "Water Delivery Service" along with organic compounds while setting the stage for the eventual evolution of life itself.

長拳者如長江大
海滔滔不絕也

—太極拳論

武當山張三丰祖師遺論

"T'ai chi ch'uan is like a great river..."

(In completing the movement *Cloudy Hands*, I recall the two great comets of my lifetime. The first of March 1996 was Comet Hyakutake; perhaps you, too, remember it as we did: "silent, bright, beautiful, a long, delicate, shining mist lofted in the dome of night." A year later, Comet Hale-Bopp would enchant millions of Earth-bound viewers for weeks.)

Water, in turn, makes me think of of waves and the rhythm of Earth's deep water cycles: evaporation, clouds, and the rains filling aquifers, streams and rivers. A line from a classic t'ai chi poem comes to mind:

"T'ai chi ch'uan is like a great river rolling on unceasingly."[105]

And, in the next movement *Fair Lady Works the Shuttles* there's a motion that imitates tidal action.[106] Tides, in turn, make me think of the moon.

The Moon

The moon, one could say, is the "child of the Earth;" that is, it was literally blasted out of Earth's crust by a Mars-sized collision some 4.5 billion years ago.[107] Yet one could also say that the moon is the "Guardian" of our Earth in the sense that it was (and is) essential for stabilizing our planet's tilt. Without the moon, Earth would radically swing about like an out of control top. Indeed, recent computer simulations indicate that without this stabilizing influence, Earth's angle of tilt would have varied between 0 and 80 degrees, (instead of its steady 23.5 degrees.[108]) Picture for a moment a tiny top wobbling uncontrollably — just before collapse. If this were our planet, Earth's climate,

> "...would have swung between epochs with extreme seasonal variations and epochs with none at all. Ecosystems very likely wouldn't have been stable long enough for advanced life-forms such as humans to evolve."[109]

A steady tilt in turn makes it possible for the steady rhythm of the seasons. Thus the next time you see the moon, perhaps from a city sidewalk on a warm summer's night, or perhaps in the chill of winter, rising above a frozen lake, think not only of the Moon's beauty, but also as "Guardian-of-Tilt," and "Giver-of-Seasons." Moonbeams, in turn, remind me of romance and of gender attraction.

Complex Life Forms

Launching a biological revolution some two billion years ago, Nature "invented" sex as a "biological insurance policy" against changing environments and also as a mechanism to keep life forms from being killed off by evolving parasites and microscopic pathogens in what one writer called "An Evolutionary Arms Race:"

> Since infectious bacteria as well a viruses and parasitic protozoans, evolve rapidly as they exploit our bodies and habits, we need to make genetic shifts in each generation to keep up with them.[110]

With sexual reproduction, multicellular life could now move ahead with new and innovative adaptive mechanisms. Consider, for example, the heart.

Whatever animal species first experienced the very earliest heart beat (approximately 800 million years ago)[111] launched a pulse through geological time, radiating outward through individuals and species, each generation keeping that primal pulse alive, like an Olympic torch-bearer, a rhythm that continues on to you and me.

Also, with each t'ai chi movement, I become more and more aware of my breath. From an evolutionary standpoint, the "invention" of lungs came relatively recently — approximately 400 million years ago.[112] Like a super-charged carburetor, lungs would have had the effect of providing early lung-fish species with more oxygen and therefore more energy for swimming or, in some cases, moving around on primitive limbs. Then, around 370 million years ago, one or several species of tetrapods (four-limbed animals) became capable of leaving the sea to make their way over a terrestrial landscape of Devonian swamps, bogs, and forests.

Bipedialism

Much later, new possibilities for our own early ancestors opened up when, during the Miocene epoch (5-23 million years ago), a climate shift began to bring major cooling and drying cycles, slowly changing dense forests into savanna-like conditions across parts of Africa. Then, approximately six to seven million years ago, some species of arboreal hominoid primate evolved a two-legged mode of locomotion (bipedalism), a trait which would later became a key to survival on the hot, dry savanna. One clear benefit of an upright stance is that it minimizes solar exposure. (For example, research shows that when all other aspects of body shape are equal, quadrupeds *gain* 60 percent more solar heat than an animal standing on two legs. Thus, a two-legged primate is capable of lowering its water requirements — a definite plus on a water-scarce savanna.[113])

Upright stance also meant the freeing up of our ancestors' hands — perfect for carrying things, fashioning artifacts and, if necessary, throwing things with keen skill and deadly accuracy. Instead of having to *biologically* adapt to new environmental challenges, we now could survive climatic changes, new dangers and other challenges with powerful *cultural* adaptations including early tools, language,[114] rituals, art, and other innovative patterns of relationships that solidified social cohesiveness.

I have an image of some savanna ancestor of mine using his or her upright stance to literally *spin around*, perhaps for surveillance, or for defense, or like an Olympic skater, for the sheer joy of it. Surprisingly, near the end of the Yang t'ai chi short form, there is, remarkably, a reminder of that antique thrill called *Turn the body and Sweep the Lotus*. Originally meant to be a martial arts defensive motion, the body swoops around as a T'ai Chi Master described it, "like a tornado."[115]

Glaciers

Consider now the rhythm of the comings and goings of major glaciation periods, the latest being some 75,000 to 12,000 years ago.

That event stimulated cold weather adaptations including cave draw-ings and carvings, plus new forms of dwellings, weapons, rituals and stories new and old, told and retold around the campfires under the skies of the Upper Paleolithic night. When the last glacier receded (12,000 to 10,000 years ago), there was another expansive pulse in the form of domestication of plants and animals, surpluses of grain, expanding agricultural technology, plus the advent of cities and civi-lizations. And then, as if we wished to keep the cosmic music in play, we "invented" music and musical instruments. Small flutes , for example, have been found in China that date back some 9000 years— each is made out of the wing bone of a Red-Crowned Crane.[116] Unbelievably, one of these ancient bird-bone flutes is still playable! Thus, in my next-to-last movements: *Step Forward, Deflect Downward, Parry, and Punch*, I softly hum a simple tune, an ancient Chinese folk song called "Xiao Bai Cai" or "Little Cabbage" which Chinese flutist Taoying Xu recorded on one of these 9000 year-old instruments. Regarding this unusual find, one member of the archeo-logical discovery team commented:

> It is important in considering the possible role of these flutes in Neolithic society to recall that ancient Chinese tradition held that there were strong cosmological connections with music: that music is part of nature.[117]

Next, consider the flowering of the great trans-tribal world reli-gions of the past 5000 years: Hinduism, Judaism, Taoism, Buddhism, Confucianism, Christianity, and Islam. Then comes the meteoric rise of scientific understandings of the last 500 years.

In the 20th Century, the "ten-thousand things" now literally *explode* in number and complexity with the advent of electricity, cars, man-made chemicals, the perfection of mechanized war, scientific medicine, space flight, computers, telecommunications, genetic-engi-neering, and the seemingly unstoppable force of a uniform globalized "Culture."

I sense a strange *unnaturalness* to these social and technologi-cal innovations, not a gentle t'ai chi pulse but (as we noted in previous chapters), an explosive blast, a turbo fire-powered ultra-*yang* rush, leaving in its path the collapse of healthy, local cultures, ecological degradation, political and economic insecurity and, from a psychological perspective, new pathologies deriving from today's pervasive technological civilization.

"Circling Hands"

Thankfully, the completion of the t'ai chi form calms my mind and body as my hands make a large circle up then into a *Cross Hands* position over my chest. There is a brief pause. Finally my hands float down to their original resting position.

In this last movement, I feel as if I were reversing *evolution*,[118] a devolution of going back in time and then ending up precisely at my starting point: *Wu Chi*, The Great Void, or original stillness. Thus, from a Taoist point-of-view, T'ai Chi's choreography is, not linear but *circular*. And after briefly (*playfully*) witnessing the universe's "Evolutionary Story," it is possible to come back home, to the wonder of the Tao as you "empty yourself of everything..."

> ...let your mind rest in peace. The ten thousand things rise
> and fall while the Self watches their return. They grow and
> flourish and then return to the source.[119]

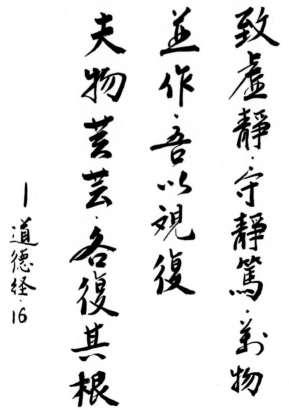

"Let your mind rest in peace..."

復命曰常

知常曰明

不知常妄作凶

—道德経、16

"If you don't realize the source..."

Chapter VI
The Wonder of the Tao

If you don't realize the source,
you stumble in confusion and sorrow...
Immersed in the wonder of the Tao,
you can deal with whatever life brings you,
and when death comes, you are ready. [120]

Lao Tzu, *Tao Te Ching*

Stillness.

Mindfulness. And now, like the roots of a flower absorbing a gentle rain, can you become *porous*, opening up — like a rebirth — to the "wonder of the Tao," the creative Power that drives the cosmos and *feel fully connected to its manifestations*?

For myself, its manifestations are like a simple flower—four petals, four different colors. Take a moment, if you wish, to color the drawing below:

Brown*

The lower petal represents our cosmological and biological past. As described in the last chapter, we all belong to a noble lineage of a cosmic/chemical and genetic/animal parentage. Each of us contains atomic structures formed in the life and death rhythm of countless stars. In addition, each of our cell's DNA is packed with deep-time animal histories—from primitive sponges to Cambrian chordates, from fish to amphibians, from reptiles to fist-sized mammals, from arboreal apes to savanna-dwelling *Homo habilis*.

Evidence of our common past is contained in our shape, our organs, our limbs, indeed in the very structure of our brains.[121] They are "shadows of forgotten ancestors" as Carl Sagan and Ann Druyan called them in their book of the same title.[122] Colored *brown*, this flower's petal represents our species' physical and psychological origins grounded in nature and Earth's long evolutionary history. It is surely a manifestation of who we *were* — and in some ways, I believe, connected to our *present* psychological well-being.

Those, for example, who live in "bubbles" of man-made technologies may find it difficult to reconnect to this ancient, "animal" part of ourselves—to experience what biologist E.O. Wilson has termed *biophilia* — an *innate* potential for psychologically bonding with nature[123]: its landscapes, ecosystems, and its communities of plants and animals. Cocooned in our cars or cooped-up in our classrooms (or office cubicles), or simply consuming hours of our waking days wandering through an unnatural wasteland of prepackaged electronic entertainments, we may be allowing this vital connection to atrophy and thereby suffer from a *peculiar loneliness*, a vague unsettling or alienation, or even depression. Children (especially) need generous chunks of unprogramed, spontaneous time in nature to discover landscape-niches "to practice the wild" as poet Gary Snyder called it.[124] Essayist Diane Ackerman agrees: "We need a lively, bustling natural world so we can stay healthy" and then adds:

*****

*The four colors — brown, yellow, red, and blue — come from the coloring pattern of a *yin/yang* quilt which can be seen on the front cover.

We need it to feel whole. We evolved as creatures knitted into the fabric of nature, and without its intimate truths, we can find ourselves unraveling.[125]

Biophilia is but perhaps a new term paralleling older themes embedded in writings that go as far back as 2nd Century naturalist, Pliny the Elder (who, for example, believed that "the only virtuous life was one lived in balance — *ratio* — with nature"[126]), the *Bible*, British poet William Wordsworth, John Muir, Aldo Leopold, and the 19th Century writer and naturalist Henry David Thoreau, to name a few.

For example, Thoreau wrote that there could be "no black melancholy to him who lives in the midst of nature and has his senses still."[127]   And what better definition of *biophilia* than Thoreau's description of an inner musical counterpoint between himself and his feathery neighbors:

> Instead of singing like the birds, I silently smiled at my inces-
> sant good fortune. As the sparrow had its trill, sitting on the
> hickory before my door, so had I my chuckle or suppressed
> warble which he might hear out of my nest...I am no more
> lonely that a single mullein or dandelion in a pasture, or a
> bean leaf, or sorrel, or a horse-fly, or a humblebee.[128]

Consider too Wisconsin writer and naturalist Aldo Leopold. Despite Leopold's training as a "bottom-line" forester, his understanding and appreciation of the natural world would eventually evolve toward values beyond economic utility, even beyond the aesthetic dimension:

> Our ability to perceive quality in nature begins, as in art, with
> the pretty. It expands through successive stages of the beau-
> tiful to values as yet uncaptured by language.[129]

Like Thoreau, Leopold would become more and more critical of an economic system geared to short-term gain and too often out of balance with ecological values. Yet by the time society evolves a true environmental consciousness, it may be too late.

Naturalist and conservationist John Muir also dedicated his energies "to do something for wildness and make the mountains glad."[130] Like Thoreau, Muir could dissipate despondency and depression by taking periodic pilgrimages into the wild.[131] My favorite quote however is not from Muir's legendary mountain hiking stories,[132] but from a moment of relaxed repose (like t'ai chi's "expansiveness") when he stretched out between two rivers and a flowering grassland:

> Here is a calm so deep, grasses cease waving...wonderful how completely everything in wild nature fits into us, as if truly part and parent of us. The sun shines not on us, but in us. The rivers flow not past, but through us, thrilling, tingling, vibrating every fiber and cell of the substance of our bodies, making them glide and sing.[133]

Judeo-Christian Environmentalism

In the same spirit as these American naturalists, major Judeo/Christian figures—Moses, John the Baptist, Jesus—apparently felt that same urge to seek spiritual nourishment in wilderness settings including rivers, lakes, mountains, and deserts. (Could, I wonder, the spiritual value of wilderness someday bring the political forces of conservative Christians together with The Wilderness Society?)

Also, as noted earlier,[134] there are compelling Biblical passages containing what could only be described as inspired environmental insight.[135] For example, what better definition of an "environmentalist" than she or he who feels an affinity with the God of *Genesis* who clearly regards the Earth with love and a sense of *great preciousness*? "God saw every thing that he had made and behold, *it was* very good."[136]

Environmentalists also share that same elation (in respect to the creation of the Earth), as described in the *Book of Job*, where

> *"...the morning stars burst out singing and*
> *the angels shouted for joy!"*[137]

Environmentalists also wish to "serve" and "keep" the "Garden"[138] (a metaphor for pristine nature), are dedicated to a "Rare Earth Covenant" and therefore committed to following God's command to Noah (*Genesis* 6:19-22) to try to save *all* animal species, i.e., "every creeping thing of the earth." As of yet, no one has discovered a commentary or footnote offering "exemptions" based on an animal's inferiority or low economic utility — whether they are flatworm or frog, rodent or snake, gorilla or human. And neither Henry Thoreau nor Aldo Leopold could describe our planet's grand magnificence better than the Psalmist as if shouting from a mountain top: "Oh Lord, how manifold are thy works! In wisdom hast thou made them all: *the earth is full of thy riches,*"

..the glory of the Lord shall endure for ever.[139]

For Bartholomew I (contemporary Ecumenical Patriarch of the Eastern Orthodox Church), any destruction or "crime" against the natural world ("the glory of the Lord") should be "considered a sin;" he then adds—in the spirit of the great poet/naturalists — that "human beings and the environment form a seamless garment of existence, a complex fabric that we believe is fashioned by God."[140]

Simplicity & Contentment

In addition, environmentalists applaud Jesus' (and St. Francis') core value of *simplicity* — not so different from Thoreau's major theme in *Walden* — and to seek *contentment*, economic and otherwise.[141] Recall too the familiar warning: "the love of money is the root of all evil."[142] Furthermore, no ecologist could have fashioned a better metaphor for a modest and sustainable life-style than Jesus' metaphor of "the lilies of the field" (Matthew 6:28):

> Consider the lilies of the field, how they grow; they toil not, neither do they spin: And yet I say unto you. That even Solomon in all his glory was not arrayed like one of these.

Wood Anemone (*Anemone quinquefolia*)

Most likely, the referred to flower is what botanists today call the "Crown Anemone" (*Anemone coronaria*) still common in northern and central Israel.[143]

As I type these words, it is early May in Wisconsin, time to check out our own version of the genus *Anemone*. In a nearby woods, I should have no trouble finding the Wood Anemone (*Anemone quinquefolia*). Friend of the Woodfern and Starflower, neighbor to the Nodding Trillium and Wild-Lily-of-the-Valley, our Wood Anemone rises only a few inches above the leaf litter. Simple, yet exceptionally beautiful, it is adorned with showy white, petal-like sepals, and a globular white stamen. (John Greenleaf Whittier once praised this diminutive beauty, shimmering in the lightest of breezes: "...wind-flowers sway/ Against the throbbing heart of May."[144]) And like the Biblical Crown Anemone, our Anemone is also lovely without effort and "fairer than Solomon in all his glory."

Native to its woodland setting, *Anemone quinquefolia* has evolved a perfect ecological "fit" to its environment, enjoying a natural balance with the other native plants and animals of its woodland "economy." In such a stable setting, ecologists are able to identify *natural checks and balances* preventing any single species from "taking over" as happens elsewhere with aggressive, invasive plants that have gained a tenacious foothold in North America: European Buckthorn, Kudzu, Oriental Bittersweet, Spotted Knapweed, Garlic Mustard, or Purple Loosestrife to name but a few.

Finally, the Wood Anemone has created a miniature "sustainable economy" humbly adding modest quantities of leaf and flower litter to the woodland floor, thereby contributing small, but reliable quantities of humus each year to our topsoil. Like Jesus' Crown Anemone, our Anemone's ecological footprint is not negative, but *positive*. The flower's nectar attracts and feeds a variety of insects (the one I saw recently was unusually thin, a couple of millimeters long and sporting an orange stripe down its back). For many flowering spring "ephemerals," their seeds are removed by ants and taken to an underground nest. There, a small portion of the seed is removed to supply protein-rich food for the ant-colony's larvae.[145] In such a form of "mutualism," the ants "return the favor" by dispersing little packets of Anemone seed-life throughout the woods.

Another way of looking at Matthew 6:28 is that Jesus' flower metaphor has captured a *"yin"* balance to the Christian message — reminding us that our spiritual life will be healthier, more whole when we can, at times, shift our attention *back to earth*. Indeed, I believe that any religion that does not harmonize Heaven *and* Earth, the "Holy Spirit" along with the "spirit of the valley," any tradition that forgets about wild flowers, or vernal pools, mudflats and soils, will become as unbalanced and dangerously "wobbly" as an economics devoid of ecological values. The Old Testament Psalmist who could write so beautifully of the "Heavenly" *yang* dimension:

> "Because thou hast made the Lord, which is my refuge,
> even the most High, thy habitation.[146]

perhaps should have added an equally true *yin counterbalance*:

> Because thou hast made nature, which is *also* my refuge,
> Even unto the most *low*, thy habitation.

Yellow

If the Earth connection is colored brown, let's color our spiritual potentialities yellow. Yellow represents the energy of the "Holy Spirit" in Christianity, Tao's Great "Being" described as

> *Wonderful, perfect...*
> *All life comes from it.*
> *It wraps everything with its love as in a garment...*
> *I do not know its name.*[147]

Or Buddhism's "Great Love" (or Great Compassion– *mahakaruna*),[148] or the *infinite* mercy of Allah[149] and Islam's "Golden Rule" (surprisingly similar to that of the Christianity and Judaism):

有物混成·先天地生

寂兮寥兮·獨立不改

周行而不殆·可以為天

下母·吾不知其名·

—道德經·25

"Wonderful, perfect..."

No one of you is a believer until he desires for his brother
that which he desires for himself.[150]

"While we know not definitely what the ultimate purport of life
is," wrote the late Zen Buddhist, T.D. Suzuki, "there is something in it
that makes us feel infinitely blessed in the living of it and remain quite
contented with it in all its evolution."[151] Yellow is the mystical awareness ballooning up and around American poet Walt Whitman as
described in his poem, "Song of Myself:"

> Swiftly arose and spread around me the peace and knowledge
> that pass all argument of the earth...And I know the spirit of
> God is the brother of my own.[152]

Yellow and brown. "Heaven and Earth." Now imagine each of
these informing the *cultural* manifestation (the third or "red" petal of
our flower).

Red

Culture is the *learned* social "force-field" we live in, influenc-
ing us all day by day, year by year, informing us not only how to survive, but how to enjoy a richer existence. If the culture's influence is
positive, it assists us in diminishing our selfishness and ego, making it
possible to move into wider circles of belonging.

Historically, traditional cultures also became very close to, even
intimate with, a particular landscape. Like the ecological "fit" of the
Anemone, many small-scale communities "fit" into their particular
locality and evolve sustainable practices and long-run economic productivity *without overshooting their carrying capacity.* For thousands
of years, successful horticultural and hunter/gatherer cultures have
integrated ecological and spiritual ethics through ceremony, cosmolo-
gies, mythologies, taboos, stories, initiations, songs, dances, food sharing, and other rituals. Overlaying specific geographical landscapes, we
therefore discover unique and sustainable "culturescapes" in all their
variation and richness.

Consider, for example, the traditional horticulturists and herders of Ladakh living in northern India artfully described in Helena Norberg-Hodge's study *Ancient Futures*.[153] In this compelling ethnography, we learn about a culture that has successfully created a mosaic of economics and values that effectively uses local resources within a system guided by Buddhist ethics — including the principles of interdependence and a reverence for life. As a professional economist, I am impressed by Ladakh's "solution" to fundamental survival problems that *all* societies face in one way or another. Ladakh's lessons have therefore become a useful, indeed an inspiring "touchstone" for me to compare and contrast with our own capitalist system.

For example, Ladakh is not a growth economy, *but a stable economy*, successfully fitting into the natural limits of its boundaries without radically altering the land or destroying its resource base. It is a landscape that not only provides economic sustenance, but is also replete with plant and animal "teachers," sacred places, and for those attuned, "patches of love and belonging."

In contrast, global capitalism *reshapes the land* without the love or belonging. Not fitting *into* the landscape, global capitalism reconfigures its landscapes based on the dictates of unlimited growth and profit — giving rise to industrial farmers, sulfide miners, stream straighteners, road wideners, wetland drainers, and forestry clear-cutters, to name a few.

In Part Two of *Ancient Futures*, Norberg-Hodge describes some of the tragic environmental and psychological impacts of Western globalization, education, and tourism on Ladakh's traditional culture. Within only two decades, the author witnessed an increase of relative poverty, social isolation, greater levels of air and water pollution, disempowerment (especially among women) and even an unexpected increase in ethnic tensions between the Buddhists and Muslims.

As traditional cultures are undermined by the seduction of "modernization" beamed out by the ubiquitous global media — billboards, movies, radio, TV, young people feel that irresistible "tug" toward Western consumptive life-styles. Shunning traditional ways, they are not completely "modern" either and therefore find themselves without sufficient income to match the promise. They're *floating in a kind of no-man's land* — unsuccessful two-worlders as it were — between traditionalism and Western "middleclassism." In some countries they are called "Hungry Ghosts."[154] Without roots in either world and without religious/cultural infrastructures of meaning and belonging (yet eager for the fruits of global consumerism) many young people become resentful and not surprisingly, prey to scapegoating and militant propaganda. Some, unfortunately, become recruits for terrorism, willing to make sacrifices that would have been unthinkable within the stable traditional culture. Understood this way, the rise of terrorism can be understood as the "underside" of globalization, economic competition, and the impact of Westernization on traditional, local cultures.

After reading Norberg-Hodge's account of Ladakh's recent stresses and struggles, I began to wonder if we too — seemingly integrated into a modern consumer economy — do not also suffer from some of the same social and psychological symptoms of land and culture uprootedness, and also experience some of the same alienation of "Hungry Ghosts" in the Third World. "And so we have before us the spectacle of unprecedented 'prosperity'" farmer/poet Wendell Berry once wrote,

> ...but in a land of degraded farms, forests, eco-systems, and water-sheds, polluted air, failing families, and diminishing communities.[155]

Hungry Ghosts can materialize in any society that "trades-in" a balanced ecological, cultural, and spiritual ethic for one obsessed with materialism, fueled by economic discontent. They thrive in an environment of pop-culture saturated with advertising and individualized electronic pre-packaged entertainments. In recognizing the "Hungry Ghost" within ourselves, we too must learn to rediscover our cultural "red petaled" rootedness. We need to become intimate with our watershed and to learn its stories and songs,[156] its geology, the names of its plants and animals, instead of, for example, media-celebrities, corporate logos, and brand names.[157] Finally, we need to develop rituals, to create (or revive) *local* crafts and folklore — indeed, to become "native to one's place," nourished by the living landscape and its "patches of love and belonging."

For example, in his book *Miracle Under the Oaks*, Richard Stevens describes some of the accomplishments, disappointments, and joys of a North Chicago based savanna/prairie restoration group. As I read between the lines, I can make out the beginnings of a true local culture evolving, informed by indigenous purpose and group solidarity, including rituals (e.g., burning the prairie in the springtime!), and by "elders" i.e., those who've mastered the art and science of ecological restoration. In a revealing comment, one member of the group said:

> What's happening here is that Europeans are finally becoming Americans. We are developing a intimate relationship with this continent, and the landscapes of the continent, and we're doing it using the science of ecology, a product of our own culture...[158]

Blue

Instead of Hungry Ghosts, there is no reason why we cannot try to become what might be called "*successful two worlders.*" First, rooted in our locality, but also comfortably at home within the broader "Culture of Learning" that includes the fruits of past and present human accomplishments — the sciences, literature, music, arts, languages. That Culture also means moving toward a "tolerance of differentness," of being open to multi perspectives plus an appreciation of selective technologies that have proven to be democratic, humane, ethical, and sustainable. Color this petal *blue*, the pastel blue of a predawn sky before sunrise, as if eager for a new day and energized by a passion to learn. It is the delight of unlimited discovery and the irrepressible spirit of free inquiry.

"The curve of a bamboo leaf..."

Liberal learning is our species' relatively new source of kinship and belonging, shining brightly through vast chunks of time and space. Despite human greed and destructiveness, despite unpardonable violence, the remarkable achievements of humankind make me glad to be a member of that quirky hominid, *Homo sapiens.*

The whole flower (and its colored petals) is, metaphorically, one way of understanding ourselves. Indeed, such a composite of my own life seems, at times, to be truly a miracle as *you* are or (in *their* own special ways) a pine tree, or a woodland flower, or the Blue Bird that just dived into the grass outside my window, or the curve of a bamboo leaf, the *sound* of a raindrop, or the virtuosity of a sunbeam! Or those mushrooms of Chapter I — *live* mushrooms that sprang up that day — so moist and cool against my cheek.

Death
Eventually, of course, new conditions arise, old ones disappear. At one moment, the wonder of the Tao's ten-thousand things takes on one face, then another and another. It was therefore not surprising when I returned to my "mushroom site" a week later, to discover that all eleven mushrooms had disappeared. Pfffft...gone! Nearby was a fern, a fragment of a Blue Jay feather, decaying pine needles, a tuft of green moss, bits of bark, rabbit dung, and a pine cone half-stripped to the core. But the mushrooms were nowhere to be seen.

Symbolically, I see my own *life* as the four-petaled flower *turned and coiled* — like a *yin/yang* diagram — *ready for movement.*[159] Likewise I see my death as the corolla relaxing its tension, its petals "letting go," disintegrating while all of its elements dissipate ever outward. For example, our brown petal will move on (like the mushrooms). One's physical body disappears into the grass, into the soft moss and down into the roots of trees. In the mind of a naturalist, death is simply the painless and beautiful merging back into the Earth. (Toward the end of his life, John Muir wrote that he saw death as nothing more than the quiet voice of Nature, a "kind nurse," whispering "...come, children, to bed, and get up in the morning — a gracious Mother calling her children home."[160])

Wood Fern

Similarly, ecologist David Abram writes that many indigenous peoples understand death as simply entering a *different dimension of life* existing within a new sphere of influence:

> ...death initiates a metamorphosis where in the person's presence does not 'vanish' from the sensible world (where would it go?), but rather remains as an animating force within the vastness of the landscape, whether subtly, in the wind, or more visibly, in animal form.[161]

Inherent in this view is the fact that the body dies, yes, but something still remains as tenderly described in the following African poem informing us that "those who are dead are never gone,"

> They are there, in the thickening shadow.
> The dead are not under the earth.
> They are in the tree that rustles,
> They are in the wood that groans.
> They are in the water that runs.
> They are in the water that sleeps...
> They are in the breast of the woman.
> They are in the child who is wailing.[162]

Of course our children also become part of our "continuation" too, where the parent's germ cells transmit living genetic material into the next generation. This continuation, however, comes at the cost of the body's death. Indeed, according to cell-biologist Ursula Goodenough, death is a "bargain made and trade-off accepted" in return for nature making it possible to evolve complex organisms of various shapes, sizes, and modalities of behavior (including, of course, ourselves). In her book, *The Sacred Depths of Nature*, Goodenough explains the difference between our biological somatic cell function (providing us with bodies that strategize for survival and reproduction and subject to change through the living/dying process of natural selection), and our *germ* cells that live on into and through future generations. In response to the question: "Does death have meaning?" Goodenough suggests an answer that is not only scientifically accurate, but in some ways optimistic as well:

Well, yes, it does. Sex without death gets you single-celled algae and fungi; sex with a mortal soma gets you the rest of the eurkayotic creatures. Death is the price paid to have trees and clams and birds and grasshoppers, and death is the price paid to have human consciousness, to be aware of all that shimmering awareness and all that love.[163]

(From a macro-evolutionary point of view, the biologist might therefore proclaim: "Long live death".)

Next, the red petal loosens its tension and radiates outward too. It is manifested in the form of one's contribution to the health of family, community and culture as well as to the health of one's local landscape: parenting, teaching, mentoring, politicking, defending wildlife, or perhaps, restoring a prairie, a watershed, a woodland, or a degraded wetland or estuary. In this sense, we are all "ancestors to generations still to be born" as one writer put it.[164] And like the potential of any action (such as a single, simple act of kindness), the "local" ripples ever outward into the global *blue zone* of uncharted times and places. Revising the popular dictum "Act locally, think globally," one might also say:

"Act locally as if it mattered globally."[165]

The yellow (spirit) petal also dissipates. But to where? (Surely it is an adventure worth looking forward to.) Do we return to the Great Void or perhaps experience the Buddhist version of rebirth?[166] Or does our consciousness merge with the energy of the Great Spirit[167] or with God into the "Kingdom of Heaven?"[168] Or are we (our souls) united with the Hindu supreme Reality—Brahman?[169]

Out of the flowage of our life and death, out of our modest receivings and givings, out of our physical bodies manifested here yet destined to move on, Lao Tzu (as if lost in wonder), drops his own tantalizing hint

*"...that all eventually will come to Tao,
as streams and torrents flow into the sea."*[170]

"Tao"

Appendix I
"Song of Ascending Yio Zhou Hill"
by
Zi-ong Chen
(661-702 A.D. Tang Dynasty)

****

Where are all the ancestors who I never met, never encountered?
Where are all those in the Universe who will come after me,
Those whom I will never know?
Contemplating infinite time and the immense Cosmos,
I shed tears for my great loneliness
And the grand wonder of it all.

End Notes

1. Lao Tzu, *Tao Te Ching*, trans. by Stephen Mitchell (New York: Harper Perennial, 1988), p. 16.
2. Quoted in Michael Adam, *Wandering in Eden* (New York: Alfred A. Knopf, 1976), p. 70.
3. Peter Douglas Ward, Donald Brownlee, *Rare Earth: Why Complex Life is Uncommon in the Universe* (New York: Copernicus Books, 1999).
4. See "We are all Starstuff," *Astronomy*, Jan., 2001, p. 59.
5. *Children's Literature*, ed. E. Johnson, E. Sickels, F.C. Sayers (Boston: Houghton Mifflin, 1959), p. 74.
6. Charles Little, *The Dying of the Trees* (New York: Penguin, 1997).
7. See Jacques Leslie's "Running Dry," *Harper's Magazine*, July, 2000, pp. 37-52.
8. See "Wafting pesticides taint far-flung frogs," *Science News*, Dec. 16, 2000, p. 391.
9. Jerome Walters, "The End of Birth," *New Age Journal*, Jan/Feb, 1994, p. 65.
10. *Ibid.* p. 65.

11. See Seth Mydans' "More than 2000 Die in Floods—Swamp Towns in the Philippines," *New York Times*, Nov. 7, 1991, p. 1.
12. Lao Tzu, *The Way of Life*, trans. by Witter Bynner (New York: Capricorn Books, 1944), p. 43.
13. *Revelation* 11:18.
14. *Genesis* 1:31 (ital. added).
15. "World's First Endangered Species Act:" (term used in a lecture, "Good News for the Land," by Calvin DeWitt, Eau Claire, Wis., Apr. 10th, 2000).
16. Calvin B. DeWitt, *Earth-Wise* (Grand Rapids, MI: CRC Publications, 1994), p. 52 (ital. added).
17. Thich Nhat Hanh, *The Sun My Heart* (Berkeley: Parallax Press, 1988), pp. 66-67.
18. Thich Nhat Hanh, *The Heart of the Buddha's Teaching* (New York: Broadway Books, 1998), pp. 126-127.
19. Ray Grigg, *The New Lao Tzu* (Boston: Charles E. Tuttle Co., 1995), p. 43.

20. Soiku Shigematsu, *A Zen Forest* (New York: Weatherhill, 1981), p. 23.
21. *A Zen Forest*, p. 23.
22. *Ibid.*, p. 23.
23. Thich Nhat Hanh, *Being Peace* (Berkeley: Parallax Press, 1987), p. 65 (italics added).
24. For CO_2 information of our life-style choices, see "Cruising for Climate Change," by Janine E. Guglielmino, (*American Forests*, Summer, 2000, pp. 41-43). American Forests offer readers assistance in calculating their approximate emissions on a web site (www.american-forests.org). For example, a kilowatt of electricity produced at an average generating plant emits 1.397 pounds of CO_2. Airline travel (miles-per-gallon-per-seat) is 48 m.p.g. As an example, a single individual on a 3000 miles flight would "consume" some 62.5 gallons. At 19.694 pounds per gallon, for that flight, that would amount to 1,231 pounds of CO_2 per flyer! American Forests calculate that the average U.S. citizen is responsible for about 10 tons of CO_2 per year which, incidently, can be offset by an annual planting of approximately 30 trees.
25. Charles E. Little, *The Dying of the Trees* (New York: Penguin Books, 1995), p. 35.
26. *Ibid.*, pp. 25-26, 35.
27. See, for example, two very informative books on this subject: Richard C. Porter's *Economics At the Wheel* (San Diego: Academic Press, 1999) and Katie Alvord's *Divorce Your*

Car! (Gabriola Island, B.C., Canada: New Society Press, 2000).

28. Ray Grigg, *The New Lao Tzu* (Boston: Charles E. Tuttle, 1995), p. 71.

29. Based on *Luke* 9:24. (Note the more familiar translation from the King James Bible: "For whosoever will save his life shall lose it: but whosoever will lose his life for my sake, the same shall save it.")

30. Matthew Arnold, *Essays in Criticism*, ed. By S.R. Littlewood (New York: MacMillan & Co., 1969), p. 173. Similarly, in reading Lao Tzu's work, translator Ray Grigg commented: "Any honest and thinking person who attempts to grasp its comprehensive wisdom finally reaches a condition in which all intellectual processes collapse. Out of this initial and profound confusion a unique sensitivity develops, a special feeling for the diverse complexity of things as they manifest themselves from moment to moment in the shifting field of a unified wholeness." (Ray Grigg, *The New Lao Tzu*, x).

31. B.J. Rendle, *World Timbers*, Vol. 3 (London: Ernest Benn Ltd., 1969), p 44.

32. All quotes are from Seth Mydans' article "More than 2000 Die as Floods Swamp Towns in the Philippines," (*New York Times*, Nov. 7th, 1991, pp. A1 and A8).

33. Helena Norberg-Hodge, "Economics, Engagement, and Exploitation in Ladakh," *Tricycle: The Buddhist Review*, Winter, 2000, p. 115. Norberg-Hodge's book *Ancient Futures* (San Francisco: Sierra Club Books, 1991) goes into more detail on the subject of the physical and psychological damage that often result from unregulated international trade.

34. The concept of *Ecological Footprint* was developed by Mathis Wackernagel and William Rees in their book *Our Ecological Footprint* (Gabriola Island, B.C., Canada: New Society Publishers, 1996). See also a summary of the authors' main points in Eben Fodor's *Better Not Bigger* (Gabriola Island, B.C.: New Society Publishers, 1999), p. 24.

35. Eben Fodor (see endnote above), p. 24.

36. *Ibid.*, p. 24.

37. Another example of business/productivity metaphors is the way we normally use of the word "time." As George Lakoff and Mark Johnson describe in their book *Philosophy in the Flesh* (New York: Basic Books, 1999) "...time is often conceptualized as a moneylike resource that can be wasted, spent wisely, squandered, and budgeted. Time in itself is not moneylike or even resourcelike. But it can be conceptualized that way via metaphor. Moreover, we can construct, and have constructed, institutions which that metaphor is made true..."(p. 530).

38. In his book *The Ecology of Commerce*, Paul Hawken asks us to consider the fact that we "are more often taught to identify types of cars than types of birds," or that we learn brand names (and corporate logos) instead of the names of flowers: commercial name identification vs flower name identification (Hawken estimates) is in a ratio of 100 to 1. (New York: Harper Business, 1993, p. 214).

39. Diane Dreher, *The Tao of Inner Peace* (New York: 1990), p. 81.

40. Physicians for Social Responsibility can be reached at 1101 Fourteenth St. NW, Suite 700, Washington, D.C. 20005.

41. "American Gridlock," by Phillip J. Longman; *U.S. News & World Report*, May 28th, 2001, p.

42. See, for example, "The Environment and Asthma in U.S. Inner Cities," by Peyton A. Eggleston, M.D., a paper given at the American Academy of Allergy, Asthma, and Immunology National Conference, March 1998.

43. See "What you Should know about Ozone," in *The Journal of Respiratory Diseases*, Vol 12 No. 5, May, 1991, p.228.

44. See Chapter 9 of Katie Alvord's book, *Divorce Your Car!* (Gabriola Island, B.C. Canada: New Society, Publishers, 2000). External costs, the author points out, that are only partially covered by drivers would include road services, oil production and transportation (including oil spills), parking costs, congestion costs, death and injury costs, pollution damage, sprawl,

unhealthy lifestyles, etc.

45. *Ibid.*, p. 130.

46. *Ibid.* p. 142.

47. *Ibid.* p. 145.

48. Economist Peter Huber (Manhattan Institute) writes that, in the case of highways, the grid-lock crisis is essentially a "4 hour" problem referring to highway demand only at rush-hour periods. His remedy involves a peak/off-peak highway pricing system for drivers which has been demonstrated in San Diego and Toronto Canada. See his "The Four-Hour Energy Crisis" in *Forbes*, September 17, 2001, p. 88.

49. See Ted Bernard and Jora Young's *The Ecology of Hope* (Gabriola Island, B.C.,Canada: New Society, 1997), pages 93-109 (Chapter 6, "Listening to the Forest").

50. The Menominee's sustainable forestry practice is a good example of "meadowlark economics," i.e., a kind of economics that bridges conventional economic principles, along with maintaining ecological integrity. See James Eggert, *Song of the Meadowlark*, (Berkeley: Ten-Speed Press, 1999), pages 3-7.

51. Consider the evolution of forest terminology: from "old growth forest" (creating an image of something akin to a forested "nursing home" implying a kind of uselessness—unless, of course, the trees are cut down and turned into forest products); to the term "ancient forests" which connotes greater dignity and respect (compare the term "ancient city"); and more recently we hear the term: "Cathedral Forests," implying a place for religious contemplation and inspiration. (See endnote below.)

52. "What non-natives consider *natural resources* are, to native people, *cultural resources*," says Mike Roberts, president of The Foundation for the Seventh Fire, a nonprofit organization dedicated to applying the wisdom of the world's indigenous people to environmental issues; "To a native person, a bend in the river can be the equivalent of the Sistine chapel; the weeds growing alongside the road can be life-saving medicines; mountains can be places where sacred ceremonies take place, ceremonies that are believed to hold the community and even the world together." (Katie Hennessey, "Lighting the Seventh Fire;" Michael Roberts, *Orion*, Autumn, 1996, p. 69, *ital. added*).

53. For examples and more information on the topic of "ecological services," see Gretchen C. Daily's article in *Science*, July 21st, 2000. In one illustration, Daily points to New York City's decision to improve city water supplies by spending $1.5 billion dollars to restore the Catskill mountain watershed, instead of an estimated $6 billion on new water treatment facilities.

54. The Land Institute of Salina, Kansas, since 1976, has been learning some "economic lessons from the prairie" too. More specifically, its Director (Wes Jackson) has been looking at the possibilities of human food production utilizing a modified "perennial polyculture" as an alternative to convential chemical/industrial agriculture. For more details, see Scott Russell Sanders' *The Force of Spirit* (Boston: Beacon Press, 2000), pages 45-58.

55. David Abram, *The Spell of the Sensuous* (New York: Pantheon Books, 1996), p. 272. See also pages 116-117 where Abram discusses the role of the traditional shaman who was able to gain knowledge, wisdom, and insight from the land itself. Will some future natural capitalist perhaps be an amalgam of an MBA/economist, ecologist, and shaman?

56. Quoted from Diane Dreher, *The Tao of Inner Peace* (New York: HarperCollins, 1990), p. 31

57. Quoted from "Tai chi for Health" video tape, by Terry Dunn (Healing Arts, Venice CA).

58. Gary Snyder, *The Practice of the Wild* (New York: North Point Press, 1990), p. 101.

59. Huston Smith, *The World's Religions: Our Great Wisdom Traditions* (San Francisco: Harper San Francisco, 1991), pages 214-215.

60. Da Liu, *T'ai Chi Ch'uan and Meditation* (New York: Schocken Books, 1986), p. 24.

61. Benjamin Pang Jeng Lo, *the Essence of T'ai Chi Ch'uan: The Literary Tradition*

(Richmond, CA: North Atlantic Books, 1979), p 100.

62. Quoted from the first chapter of *Tao Te Ching* trans. by Gia-Fu Feng and Jane English (New York: Vintage Books, 1972).

63. T'ai Chi Ch'uan can also be written "*taijichaun*" (taiji= yin/yang balance; plus the word chaun= "fist" or a form of martial art).

64. "Tai Chi; A Gift of Balance" is the name of a popular video by Tingsen Xu designed for senior citizens to improve their balance. See Wayfarer Publications Catalog (www.tai-chi.com).

65. Wolfgang Metzger and Peifang Shou, *Tai chi Ch'uan & Qigong: Techniques & Training* (New York: Sterling, 1996); see especially Chapter 2: "Tai chi Ch'uan & Qigong: Antidote to Today's Stress (p. 28-44).

66. Linda Myoki Lehrhaupt, *T'ai Chi As a Path of Wisdom* (Boston: Shambhala, 2001), p. 55.

67. Thich Nhat Hanh, *The Miracle of Mindfulness: A Manual on Mediation* (Boston, Beacon Press, 1975), p. 11.

68. Da Liu, *Taoist Health Exercise Book* (New York: Link Books), p.37.

69. Bob Klein, *Movements of Magic: The Spirit of T'ai-chi-Ch'uan* (North Hollywood: Newcastle Publishing, 1984), p. 28. "Direct perception" has also been described as "pure observation" by Zen practitioner Swami Nirmalananda. See *A Garland of forest Flowers* (Bombay: R.V. Raghavan, 1993), p. 25.

70. *Ibid.*, p. 27.

71. *Ibid.*, vii.

72. See Ken Cohen's web page (www.qigonghealing.com).

73. Lawrence Galante, *Tai Chi, The Supreme Ultimate* (York Beach, Maine: Samuel Weiser, 1981), p. 19.

74. Cheng Man-Cheng, *Master Cheng's New Method of Taichi Ch'uan Self-Cultivation*, trans. by Mark Hennessy (Berkeley, Frog, Lid., 1999), p. 19.

75. Neil de Grasse Tyson, *One Universe* (Washington D.C., Joseph Henry Press, 2000), p. 134-136.

76. Note that the word "Chi" as in T'ai Chi Ch'uan means "great," "limit" or "ultimate" as in the phrase "Supreme Ultimate" whereas ch'i (*qi*) means "intrinsic energy," "vital breath, or life-force."

77. Cohen, (see web page above), "What is Qigong?"

78. Kenneth S. Cohen, *The Way of Qigong* (New York: Ballantine Books, 1997), p. 271.

79. Grigg, p. 80.

80. T'ai Chi Master Chungliang Al Huang was quoted as saying, "I tell them to practice *tai ji* to understand nature, to not only talk about ecology and environmental awareness, but to embody it and use the learning in their lives." See *A Gathering of Cranes* by Solala Towler (Eugene: Abode of the Eternal Tao, 1996), p. 124.

81. Lo, p. 99.

82. Lao Tzu, *The Way of Lao Tzu (Tao-te ching)*, trans. By Wing-Tsit Chan (New York: Macmillan, 1963), p. 176.

83. N.J. Girardot, *Myth and Meaning in Early Taoism* (Berkeley: University of California Press, 1983), p. 93.

84. Max Kaltenmark, *Lao Tzu and Taoism*; trans. By Roger Greaves; (Stanford: Stanford University Press, 1965), p. 43.

85. Michael Adam, *Wandering in Eden* (New York: Knopf, 1976), p. 66.

86. Dreher, p. 32.

87. Thich Nhat Hanh, *The Heart of the Buddha's Teachings* (New York: Broadway Books, 1998), p. 24.

88. Kenneth S. Cohen, "Qigong is more than Meditation:" *T'ai Chi Magazine*, Feb. 2000,

p.33.

89. For more on Professor Cheng Man-ch'ing's version of the Yang Family Short Form, see Cheng Man Ch'ing, *Cheng Tzu's Thirteen Treatises on T'ai chi ch'uan*; tran. by Benjamin Pang Jeng Lo and Martin Inn; (Berkeley: North Atlantic Books, 1985); and also Cheng Man-ch'ing's *Master Cheng's New Method of Taichi Ch'uan Self-cultivation*, trans. By Mark Hennessy (Berkeley: Frog, Ltd. 1999).

90. Lehrhaupt, p. 27-29.
91. Cheng Man-Ch'ing, *Master Cheng's New Method of Taichi Ch'uan*; trans. By Mark Hennessy (Berkeley: Frog Ltd.,1999), p. 35.
92. Liu, p. 13.
93. Soiku Shigematsu, *A Zen Forest: Sayings of the Masters* (New York: Weatherhill, 1981), p. 76.
94. See Wayfarer Publications: P.O. Box 39938, Los Angeles, CA 90039 or www.tai-chi.com
95. Albert Einstein, *Ideas and Opinions* (New York: Wings Books, 1954), p. 11, 40, and 38.
96. Heather Couper and Nigel Henbest, *Big Bang* (New York: DK Publishing, 1997), p. 10.
97. See "Guth's Grand Guess," by Brad Lemley, *Discover*, April, 2002, p. 36; and also "A Universe from Nothing," by Alexei V. Filippenko and Jay M. Pasachoff; *Mercury*, March-April, 200,. p. 19.
98. Waysun Liao, *The Essence of T'ai Chi* (Boston: Shambhala, 1995), p. 61.
99. Lehrhaupt, p. 184.

100. Ron Cowen, "Sounds of the universe confirm Big Bang," *Science News*, April, 28, 2001, p. 261 (*ital*. added).
101. Tom Yulsman, "Give Peas a Chance," *Astronomy*, Sept. 1999, p 41.
102. Lao Tzu, *The Way of Life*, trans. By R.B. Blakney (New York: American Library, 1955, p. 56.
103. William Speed Weed, "What's Water got to do with it?"; *Astronomy*, Aug. 2001, p. 40.
104. *Ibid.*, p. 40.
105. Lo, Inn, Amacker, Foe, p. 25.
106. Lehrhaupt, p. 170.
107. See William K. Hartmann and Chris Impey's Astronomy, the Cosmic Journey (Belmont, CA: Wadsworth, 1994), p. 170-174.
108. "Moon of Our Delight," *Discover*, Jan, 1994. p. 72.
109. *Ibid.*, p. 72.

110. Mark Ridley, "Sex, Errors, and the Genome," *Natural History*, June, 2002, p. 49.
111. Carl Zimmer, "The Hidden Unity of Hearts," *Natural History*, April, 2000, p. 56.
112. *Ibid.*, p. 60.
113. Tim Folger, "The Naked and the Bipedal," *Discover*, Nov. 1993, p. 34.
114. Best guess date for the beginnings of human language is approximately 500,000 years ago. See Matt Cartmill's "The Gift of Gab," *Discover*, Nov. 1998, p. 64.
115. Man-Ch'ing, p. 184.
116. Juzhong Zhang, et al. "Oldest playable musical instruments found a Jiahu early Neolithic site in China, *Nature*, Sept. 23, 1999. The flute recording could be heard at http://www.nature.com. Note that the earliest instrument so far discovered is a small 36,000 year old bone pipe found in southern Germany. See Susan Milius' "Face the Music," in *Natural History*, Dec. 2001, p. 54.
117. *Ibid.*, p.367.
118. This is similar to Prabhavananda/Isherwood's commentary on the Yoga Aphorisms of Patanjali: "For meditation is evolution in reverse. Meditation is a process of devolution. Beginning at the surface of life, the meditative mind goes inward, seeking...the cause behind

the cause, until the innermost Reality is reached." See Patanjali, *How to Know God* (New York: New American Library, 1953), p. 28.

119. Translated by Gia-Fu Feng and Jane English; Lao Tzu, *Tao Te Ching* (New York: Vintage books, 1972, Verse # 16.

120. Mitchell, Chapter 19.

121. See *The Book of Life,* General Editor: Stephen Jay Gould (New York: W.W Norton, 2001). P. 39.

122. Carl Sagan & Ann Druyan, *Shadows of Forgotten Ancestors: A Search for Who We Are* (New York: Random House, 1992).

123. Edward O.Wilson, *Biophilia* (Cambridge: Harvard University Press, 1984).

124. Gary Snyder, *The Practice of the Wild* (New York: North Point Press, 1990).

125. "Finding a Time Pool," by Diane Ackerman, *Audubon*, Jan-Feb, 2002, p. 49.

126. "Pliny the Elder's Environmental Ethic," a presentation by Dr. Kenneth Parejko at the conference "Ecology, Theology and the Judeo-Christian Environmental Ethic," Feb. 22, 2002, Notre Dame University.

127. Henry David Thoreau, *Walden* (New York: Bramall House, 1951), p. 148.

128. *Ibid.*, p.128 and 154.

129. Aldo Leopold, *A Sand County Almanac* (London: Oxford University Press, 1949), p., 96.

130. Quoted from PBS documentary "American-1900" produced by David Grubin, 1999.

131. See Linnie Marsh's Pulitzer Prize winning biography *Son of the Wilderness: The Life of John Muir* (Madison Wisconsin: University of Wisconsin Press, `1945).

132. See, for example, *The Wild Muir: Twenty-two of John Muir's Greatest Adventures*, by John Muir; selected by Lee Stetson (Yosemite CA: Yosemite Association, 1994).

133. Quoted from Joseph Cornell's *Listening to Nature* (Nevada City, CA: Dawn Publications, 1987), p. 42.

134. See Chapter l.

135. A common criticism of the Bible by environmentalists is that it promotes *dominion* "over the fish of the sea, and over the fowl of the air, and over every living thing that moveth upon the earth." (*Gen.* 1:28) "Dominion," according to Bibilical scholar and environmental teacher Calvin B. DeWitt actually means something less destructive: "dominion is a form of steward-ship, similar to the King's duties described in *Deuteronomy* 17." The implication is therefore not *domination* but more a "loving, caring, keeping of that which one has been entrusted." (Conservation with Calvin DeWitt, Prof. Environmental Studies, University of Wisconsin, Madison).

136. *Genesis* 1:31 (King James Version).

137. *Job* 38:7. Taken from Stephen Mitchell's trans. *The Book of Job* (New York: Harper, 1979), p. 79.

138. DeWitt, p. 51. "Human beings are called to serve ('*abad*) and keep (*shamar*) the garden in the goodness and fruitfulness of God's creation (Gen. 2:15)."

139. Psalm 104:24 (*ital.* added) and 31 (King James Version).

140. "The Venice Declaration: A Spiritual Imperative for Earth Care," by Sparlha Swaby, *Earthlight*, Summer, 2002, p. 6.

141. Philippians 4:11 and 1 Timothy 6:6-9.

142. 1 *Timothy* 6:10 (King James Version).

143. Timothy Coffey, *The History and Folklore of North American Wildflowers* (Boston: Houghton Mifflin, 1993), p 10.

144. Quoted in Mrs. William Starr Dana's *How to Know the Wild Flowers* (New York, Dover Publications, 1963), p. 6.

145. Called "myrmecochorous" ants.

146. *Psalm* 91:9.
147. K.L. Reichelt, *Meditation and Piety in the Far East* (New York: Harper & Bros., 1954), p. 41.
148. See Thich Nhat Hanh's *Call Me by My True Names* (Berkeley: Parallax Press, 1999), p. 33, and also his *Fragrant Palm Leaves* (Berkeley: Parallax Press, 1998), p. 211.
149. See Matthew S. Gordon's *Islam* (New York: Oxford, 2002), p. 23.

150. Quoted from the *Sunnah* in the *Old Farmer's Almanac* (1992, p. 261).
151. D.T. Suzuki, *Zen Buddhism*, ed by William Barrett (New York: Doubleday, 1956), pp. 3-4.
152. Walt Whitman, *Leaves of Grass* (New York: Paddington Press, 1970), p. 14 (from "Song of Myself," #5).
153. Helena Norberg-Hodge, *Ancient Futures* (San Francisco: Sierra Club Books, 1992).
154. Thich Nhat Hanh, *Touching Peace* (Berkeley: Parallax Press, 1992), p. 99-100.
155. "The Idea of a Local Economy," by Wendell Berry; *Harper's Magazine*, April, 2002, page 16.
158. For an interesting description of the important of indigenous songs, see Martin Prechtel's *Secrets of the Talking Jaguar* (Tarcher/Putnam, 1998).

157. See endnote number 38.
158. Richard Stevens, *Miracle Under the Oaks* (New York: Pocket Books, 1995), p. 202.
159. See yin/yang illustration on the front cover; this is a photograph of a small quilt made by my wife, Pat Eggert.

160. Quoted in Linnie Marsh Wolfe's *Son of the Wilderness: The Life of John Muir* (Madison Wis: University of Wisconsin Press, 1945), p. 348.
161. David Abram, *The Spell of the Sensuous* (New York: Pantheon Books), p. 16.
162. Quoted from Knowledge Products' "The Religion of Small Societies" (Nashville: Carmichael & Carmichael Inc., 1994), tape 1, side 2.
163. Ursula Goodenough, *The Sacred Depths of Nature* (New York: Oxford, 1998), p. 151.
164. Quoted from Tsonakwa and Yolaikia's *Legends in Stone, Bone, and Wood* (Minneapolis: Arts and Learning Services Foundation, 1986), p. 11.
165. Suggested by my friend Paul Gruchow, author of *Grass Roots: The Universe of Home* (Minneapolis: Milkweed, 1995).
166. A Buddhist perspective on death. See *Going Home: Jesus and Buddha as Brothers*, by Thich Nhat Hanh (New York: Riverhead Books, 1999), p. 13.
167. As told to the author in conversation with Arnie Neptune (Grandfather Thunder), Penobscot Indian Elder (Concord MA, July 11th, 2002).
168. *Matthew* 5: 3 & 10.
169. See *The Song of God: Bhagavad-Gita*; trans. Swami Prabhavananda and Christopher Isherwood (New York: New American Library: 1951), p. 74.

170. Quoted from *The Spiritual Athlete: A Primer for the Inner Life*; ed. Ray Berry (Olema, CA: Joshua Press. 1992), p. 139.

About the Author

James Eggert is a writer and emeritus faculty member at the University of Wisconsin-Stout (Menomonie Wisconsin). He is the author of *What is Economics* (4th ed.) and *Song of the Meadowlark: Exploring Values for a Sustainable Future.*

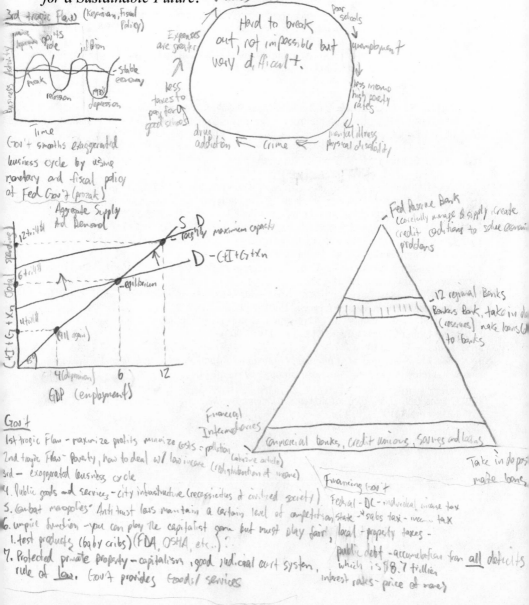

regressive tax - where poor people pay more % of their income (sales tax are regressive)
progressive tax - he who has the most financial resources, should pay the most tax

Tax philosophies

1. Benefits received - he who gets the benefit of the expenditure should pay the tax.

2. Ability to pay applies to the distribution of income perspective.

3. proportional or flat tax - everyone pays the same amount

4. Social Security tax - proportional tax up to $94,200 - if you make more than this you only have to pay up to $94,200. (wealthy pay a greater %)

1. Poverty - Basic def - The amount of $ that it takes a family to live on (4 members urban area) $19,000 poverty line

2. Relative poverty - feel poor in relation to other people around you

3. Philosophical Poverty - ratio of a persons income over desires, >1 will not feel poor <1 will feel poor
   (income / desire)

4. empowerment poverty - how much control do you have over your life?

Poverty groups
1. Aged - ppl on SS, big drug costs.
2. Feminization of poverty - single mother raising child, ? save of none
3. Innercity - Spanish speaking, Af Am's w/o resources suffer from all 4 definitions of poverty (video)
4. Rural Poor - Farmers that aren't making it.
5. Structurally unemployed - ppl thrown out of work b/c of a structural change in economy. rebate economy
6. Underclass poverty - outside of social services network, drug abuse, teenage runaways, discouraged unemployment - unsuccessful at finding work.

GDP - standard bearer of macroeconomics - total value of all goods/services produced in a yr. 12 trillion

GPI - Genuine progress indicator - subtract out the bads, add well being issues, volunteer services

Population Growth - if a population rate is 4% and GDP rate is 3%, each person is starting to be another indicator of the economy GDP per capita

5. non-market transactions - build your own home - do something for me ill do something for you
7. Distribution of income - upper echelon is receiving majority of the income # Always critique economy #
5. Price changes - common issue of inflation - inflation distorts GDP, makes it less reliable.

Real GDP - determine base yr. compare all yrs. to the base yr GDP in flation adjusted, we should be using

Inflated GDP - Money GDP - not incorporated all aspects inflated GDP

GDP price deflator - includes changes in prices of all purchases throughout the economy, gov't, business,
foreigners - Am purchases in the Am economy.

What is the proper monetary fiscal policy in times of Hyperinflation
  1. Sell bonds   opposite in times of recession
  2. raise reserve ratio
  3. raise the discount rate

  If facing hyperinflation - cut gov't spending, raise taxes (surplus policy)

Budgetary philosophies
Annual - yearly.
Cyclical - balance budget over balancing cycle
Functional - don't worry about balancing budget
Political Pragmatism - favors deficit

Printed in the United States
41936LVS00006B/40-108